Are You Chasing Rainbows?

A personal and practical insight into emotional maturity and why adults sometimes behave like children

Alison R. Russell

Balloonview

Certain names and other identifying details have been changed to protect the privacy of individuals.

Printed and bound in Great Britain by
CPI Group (UK) Ltd, Croydon, CR0 4YY

ISBN 978-1-907798-35-1

Book Cover by Neil Genge

Acknowledgements

There so many people who are responsible the different pieces that make up the whole publication of Chasing Rainbows and my deepest thanks go to them all.

Professionally, it would not have happened without Joe Griffin, Ivan Tyrrell, Julian Penton, Wendy and John Amey, Gail Rhodes, Bill Andrews, John M, Sue Hanisch, Merv Edmunds, Gwyneth Moss, Neil Genge, Ed Peppitt, Lisa Cordaro, Lisa Snape and Tanya Solomons.

Personally, I have been supported with love and constant encouragement by Adrian Leaman, Katie, Mark, Paul and Jack Kelly, Joe, Noah and Adelaide Harland, Nicola Di Tullio, Carolyn Findell, Samantha Richley, Patricia Rofe, Helen Speake, Katie Douglas and Elizabeth Stead.

I also thank all of those people that have played their part in my life, given me the inspiration for the subject matter, but were unaware of their contribution.

Thank you everyone.

October 2013

Dedication

To Sylvia and Margaret

Contents

Preface

Imagine a rainbow. It could be a memory of a real experience, or a figment of the imagination. We become lost in wonder at the rainbow's form and the spectrum of rich colours in a changing sky. We are momentarily entranced and we marvel at the rainbow's natural beauty and its transient nature.

Our eyes wander to where the end of it disappears... The image fades. It was a moment of innocent wonder and curiosity. For a few precious seconds the intrusion of our everyday activities was excluded. No harm was done. In fact, we may even feel uplifted.

Now, let us imagine another rainbow. Again, we become entranced by it, but this time we concentrate on where the rainbow ends. We remember the stories and myths we heard as children. Is there really a pot of gold at the end of the rainbow? A pot of gold that would provide a resolution to all our problems? We want it, and we want it now!

Leaving common sense and reason behind, we chase the end of the rainbow, again and again. We keep trying, but the end is just out of reach and always unobtainable. We feel disappointed, frustrated and weary. Will we ever reach it? No. The pot of gold of resolution is the delusion in the illusion, but we continue to reach for and chase the end of the rainbow. In fact, the more we try, the more we can become deluded. We can become emotionally and physically unwell.

Introduction
'Oh, grow up!'

> *But I like behaving like a child at times – it can get me what I want.*
>
> **Tom, a middle-aged colleague**

Have you ever looked at an adult and thought, "Oh grow up"? Perhaps you have uttered those precise words. I am sure you have – in fact, I should be astonished if you have not. The person may be someone well-known to you, or a complete stranger. It makes no difference to the fact that at that precise moment, their behaviour in some way resembles that of a child, and you are feeling a sense of despair and frustration.

If this person is someone who you have to live or work with, then it could be helpful to understand a little of what may be happening in their brain. Of course, in the unlikely event that those words have ever been said or thought about you, then it might be helpful to know what may be happening in your brain.

However, it is not only the expression "Oh, grow up!" that is commonly used. There are all sorts of words and phrases that suggest the speaker is observing some behaviour that they find irritating and exasperating.

"You're acting like a child/two-year-old."
"Why can't you act your age?"

"Stop being so childish."
"You're behaving like a spoilt brat."
"Your child acts older than you do."

Then there are descriptions of immature behaviour:

"They threw their toys out of the pram."
"They spat the dummy out."
"She's daddy's little princess."
"He's a mummy's boy."
"He's a Peter Pan."
"It's playground behaviour."

The type of immature behaviours that can be observed include:

- having tantrums
- sulking
- pouting
- slamming doors
- throwing things in a temper
- not facing the speaker
- blocking ears
- sucking a thumb or sleeve

In the context of this book, this is about when these expressions and descriptions are of adult behaviour. They are not complimentary, and they are used in a critical way: the implication is that the person allegedly behaving like a child is, in fact, an adult.

What precisely is being described in such a negative way? The criticism may be directed at the whole person, but really it is only a part of them that appears to be a little underdeveloped at times. Physically, they should be at their fully grown height and weight, so their build is not childish. Chronologically, they have grown to be the age shown on their birth certificate: the age of an adult. Intellectual growth may have some development to go, as we should carry on learning all our lives. One motto for healthy ageing is: 'Use it or lose it'. In 2013, the British Government suggested that the over-sixties should study degrees. Many people over 60 continue to work and learn in a variety of ways, and have been doing so for decades.

Generally, the IQ (Intelligence Quotient) is appropriate for the adult's age. Immature behaviour can appear quite incomprehensible at times if the adult we are observing is highly intelligent. So, what we are left with is emotional development (EQ or Emotional Intelligence). Could it be that while the person looks and works like an adult, at times they feel like a child and their behaviour reflects their feelings? Perhaps some of their emotions are well past their sell-by date. If some of the following statements, which have been said to me by people with emotional health problems, are true, then I suggest they are:

"I behave like a stroppy teenager."
"My mother makes me feel like a child of six."
"My father treats me like a nine-year-old."
"I'm forty-five going on five."

Think anger in children, think of a tantrum.
Think adult throwing a tantrum, think child.

After some years of seeing clients who were able to recognise their own infantile behaviours, there was one question that interested me: why do adults behave like children? What is the point? What do they gain? It doesn't seem to make anyone happy, so why do it?

I should state here that if there is a tacit agreement between adults that childish behaviour will be tolerated, then there may be no problem to address. If people in relationships are tolerant and supporting of behaviour that is carried on behind closed doors and does not upset anyone else, then this is not a criticism of them. After all, there are different strokes for different folks (Chapter 9).

Childish, or childlike?

"There's nothing wrong with being childish. It's fun." I have heard this many times from people disagreeing with my views, but they tend to be mixing up *childish* with *childlike*. The difference between childish and childlike is important and needs to be highlighted from the beginning, as the difference is not always appreciated.

Childlike

Enjoying child*like* moments of joy, fun, wonderment, innocent curiosity and simple pleasures is to be recommended and encouraged until the day we die. We can still behave as an adult and remain in control, and it is not boring. It can be delightful, uplifting, fun and enjoyable for all. I definitely recognise and enjoy childlike moments in my life. Some examples are:

- visiting the seaside
- receiving gifts
- playing games with children
- having harmless fun

Childish

What certainly is boring and a pain for everyone involved is childish behaviour. Someone behaving in a childish way appears to have had their emotions hijacked, their thoughts and actions taken over ('hijack' is a term coined by Daniel Goleman in his book *Emotional Intelligence*; see Bibliography). The results can be extremely damaging and long-lasting. For example:

- sulking and tantrums
- being disruptive
- addictive behaviour
- manipulative behaviour
- being violently possessive

Why do it?

Sometimes we feel that we have missed out on some 'magic' from childhood, and carry on looking for it through a life of dashed hopes and unfulfilled expectations. We might be able to capture some missing 'magic' only to find that it is not what we were expecting. It can't be. We are not the same people as we were then, and circumstances have changed. For that reason too, we cannot right past wrongs, real ones or perceived.

We use certain behaviours to change the behaviour of someone we are communicating with: this could be conscious or unconscious. This is the ripple effect: actions and consequences. Something will follow on from each action that we take, but it might not be what we are expecting. In babies and young children the actions are impulsive, but we gradually learn self-control and think before acting. This learned behaviour can work well until we are hijacked by an emotion attached to a memory-match, which can cause us to regress in our behaviour and actions. Again, it can be conscious or unconscious (Chapter 12).

Illustration

Our memory is like playing the card game 'Snap'. Using the five senses of sound, taste, touch, sight and smell, our brain matches what it is experiencing in the present with memories from the past. If the brain is unable to provide an exact match, then it will find the nearest thing. Hence the use of the word 'like' when we are describing something. This starts from the moment of birth. A baby will seek out something to suck. If it is not a breast, it will be something 'like' a breast. I call this game of brain snap 'memory-matching'.

If an adult's emotional brain is hijacked by an 'immature' child, they could regress to a behaviour that they used as a child when they were not getting their own way: for example, sulking, shouting or stomping away from a discussion. My suggestion is that as adults we are attempting to find resolution for the child that the adult once was: not a different child or a newly-discovered child, but the child we once were. In this book, I refer to this child as 'mini-me'. We strive endlessly for the unattainable, which no amount of sulking, hitting, yelling, throwing, seeking perfection, substance abuse or spending money will solve. In the process, the adult feels out of control, because control is in the hands of a 'mini-me'.

This immature thinking can lead to self-destructive behaviours. A classic example is the person who unconsciously looks for the resolution to a problem they had with a parent in their choice of adult partner. It can lead to frustration and unhappiness all round. Sometimes it leads to multiple relationships, as the search goes on through life. The parent does not have to have been a problem; they could be idolised. Either way, the search will still be fruitless.

This book is to help those people who are either unhappy in the situation that they find themselves in, or live and work with people who appear to be unhappy.

What is the point?

As previously stated, all behaviour achieves something, although it may be that what the behaviour achieves is not really what was wanted. The question is to examine whether there is a more mature way of behaving that causes less grief to the giver and receiver.

Why 'chasing rainbows'?

Forty-four-year-old Neil was explaining some behaviour that wasn't helping a domestic situation. There was something he had said that brought out the following response from me: "You might as well be chasing rainbows!" I explained that he was describing a situation where his goal was in fact an illusion, and he was becoming deluded and emotionally unwell in his attempts to reach it. He understood immediately. "I feel as if I've spent my life running backwards and forwards trying to fill a child's half-empty bucket, but it never gets filled."

What's my research, and where's my evidence?

I have two children and four grandchildren. I have experienced some challenging times while growing up, during my education and throughout life – a normal life. I am a trained nursery nurse with a variety of workplace experiences, including years on maternity units, in private homes, nurseries and playgroups. For most of my professional childcare years I worked with the under-fives.

I spent ten years in retail and management, and then moved to another part of the country. Agency work as a nursery nurse led to work on an acute unit in a psychiatric hospital. I stayed on as a nursing assistant, and after three years decided that there must be a more effective way of helping people and relieving them of their distress. I retrained as a psychotherapist, and in 2001 opened a private practice. I worked using a short-term, solution-focused therapy, using a variety of cognitive and behavioural therapeutic interventions. The focus was mainly on the client's unmet emotional needs and their unused or misused resources (Chapter 1 and 2). I found it a most effective way to help many people experiencing emotional health problems, including depression, stress, addiction, anxiety disorders and trauma.

However, there were some clients where something else appeared to be going on other than just missing adult needs or misusing resources. Using my nursery nursing experience, I realised that I was seeing and hearing about childish behaviour hijacking adult behaviour – repeatedly. Verbally and non-verbally. Sometimes it would appear that the adult morphed into the child in front of me.

Why did they keep repeating such childish behaviour? What were they trying to achieve? The consequences rarely appeared satisfactory, so why did they continue? Did they realise what was going on? I asked my colleagues to look for these signs, and they too reported the same findings. Although there has been healthy discussion on exactly what is happening in the mind and body, even neuroscientists and psychologists don't have all the answers, as new findings and theories are published frequently.

I have undertaken research using what I have observed, heard and read in the real world and real life. I have also used personal experiences over 60 years. Not a week goes by without a news report or magazine article containing an example of what I would describe as 'chasing rainbows' behaviour. I have never met anyone who did not recognise exactly what I was talking about – although naturally there have been disagreements about why it happens.

Family relationships can be fraught with difficulties if the child is not allowed to grow up into an adult. How many times do we hear from adults who are mature in years saying, "My parent still treats me like a child"? I would suggest that we can allow ourselves to be treated like a child by not drawing boundaries of expected behaviour (Chapter 8).

From the feedback I have received when I tell people the subject of the book, it would appear that the workplace can be full of competing 'mini-mes'. In August 2006, a City bank administrator, Helen Green, won £817,000 because she had been bullied at work – by other women, a group who constantly told her she smelled and blew raspberries at her. This is straight out of the playground. It is not so much juvenile as infantile, with results that can only lead to poorer productivity and increased sickness levels. Barely a month goes by without a political commentator writing that the House of Commons resembles a playground on occasions. The Palace of Westminster is stuffed with people who are intellectually bright – indeed, some are very intelligent – but emotionally mature? That's another matter.

The growing up process from an emotionally incontinent child to an emotionally mature adult need not be painful: no growing pains here. Relief is the most frequently expressed emotion, although there can be secondary gain from not changing behaviours (Chapter 18). The realisation of what has been happening in our lives, and that we can take control instead of losing it, can be liberating. Very few tears are shed in the processing of growing up.

The recognition of childish behaviour in adults has been well documented and researched over many decades. Transactional Analysis's 'inner child' uses these findings, as does Neuro-Linguistic Programming's 'timeline' work. Hypnosis uses 'the affect bridge' and regression. The psychologists Oliver James and Dorothy Rowe are among many who have written a number of books about the adult–child dynamic in family situations. An American psychologist, Pauline Wallin, has written a book called *Taming Your Inner Brat*. Brandon Bays uses 'The Journey'. There is Michael Bywater's *Big Babies* book, the media use of the word 'kidults' and so on. A problem of emotional immaturity has been identified and the presence of a child in some form inhabiting an adult's mind has been acknowledged.

However, I believe that there has been something missing in the understanding of why the child is sometimes present. I do not believe our child is a brat. I suggest that this child is sometimes a very frightened, even traumatised child. Fear is the baseline emotion (Chapter 11). As children we may have felt sad, scared, angry and/or bewildered. Could this be because our needs were not met when we were children, and we didn't feel good enough to get them met? Perhaps, through misuse of the imagination and a child's simple understanding of the world around them, we perceived a situation incorrectly (Chapter 15).

Illustration

We all need money to live, but Maggie was fearful of being without it, and this limited her enjoyment of life. As a small child, she recalled her mother continually saying to her father, "We'll all end up in the gutter," and she believed it, literally.

In practice I have found that in the main, those unmet needs are one or more of the following: attention, security, love, friendship, feeling valued and achievement. I believe that as a child there was a time when we did not feel good enough. Not good enough to be loved. Not good enough to be a friend. Not good enough at school. Not good enough to be valued. Not good enough in the family. Not good enough to be thought competent.

The message that many adults carry around like a yoke, is one that states: "I am not good enough to get my needs met." It is a phrase that will be a thread through this book. The chapters will explain how a lack of meeting emotional needs can manifest itself in a multitude of behaviours. Of course, it is impossible to turn the clock back, so the result can be one of continual disappointment and often a deterioration in emotional health.

We grow up, but mini-me can continue to hijack us. As an adult, we attempt to 'make it better' for mini-me and can continue to try for decades – a hopeless task, like chasing rainbows. The simple truth is that mini-me cannot get its past needs met in the present, no matter how hard we try.

Conversely, perhaps our needs were met, but in ways that we should have outgrown as adults. Clients talk of sulking, tantrums and a diverse range of attention and validation-seeking behaviours. All these could have got our needs met as children, but sometimes prove to be problematic when used in the same way when we are adults.

Therapists have found that many people are readily able to identify their childish behaviour. Other people have realised what is happening after some gentle information-gathering. I should add that most of us are capable of a little self-awareness (Chapter 19), and perhaps recognise that the motivation behind some of our behaviours is not always to satisfy the adult self. I have identified that my own mini-me is a ten-year-old full of a sense of injustice with authority figures: it often used to hijack me in workplace situations. No wonder the outcomes were not helpful, and made me even more indignant. It is embarrassing to think about it. I still feel that sense of injustice at times, but manage the situation in a more mature manner.

As children, we should be guided and set boundaries by our parents and teachers. As adults we need to be doing it for ourselves (Chapter 8). There is a chance that in fact – and this might be embarrassing to admit – someone has expressed frustration with your own behaviour. Perhaps you are not really happy about it, although you may be loath to acknowledge that fact. You may not really like yourself much. Read the book and see if you have any personal 'lightbulb moments'.

On my desk I have a coaster. It has this saying on it, which is attributed to Buddha:

> Believe nothing, no matter where you read it or who has said it, not even if I have said it, unless it agrees with your own reason and your own common sense.

I cannot ask for any more from the reader.

Chapter 1

'I need it, really really need it':

needs and wants

Children are completely egoistic; they feel their needs intensely and strive ruthlessly to satisfy them.

Sigmund Freud

It makes me smile when I pass a small child in a shop, looking pleadingly at the adult they are with, saying or shouting "I really need it!"; maybe they are accompanied by a doe-eyed look, a pouting mouth or flowing tears, or perhaps a foot being stamped. As adults, we know that they don't really need it – they just want it, but don't know the difference. It is hard to resist, and adults do not always stand their ground. It seems so easy to give into the demands and perhaps save an embarrassing scene in the shop: short-term gain, but long-term pain.

What about an adult who behaves like that? These words have been heard many times over the years: "I don't really know why I feel like this, I have everything I want." "Perhaps", I have replied, "but do you have everything you *need*?"

My therapeutic work was focused on the emotional needs that a person has, and the skills and abilities that nature has given them to get these needs met. These needs will be referred to throughout the book, and are the foundations for my interpretation of the observations made:

- Love – loving and being loved
- Attention – giving and receiving attention
- Personal value – feeling good enough
- Privacy – having one's own space
- Safety – feeling secure
- Control – feeling a sense of control
- Achievement – succeeding while being stretched
- Friends – for fun and friendship
- Social group – being part of one

There is still a stigma attached to the subject of mental health. Whatever people may think, the situation is not as bad as it used to be, when the very mention of someone having mental health problems – maybe a family member – would have been taboo. Nowadays, everyone knows someone who has experienced a mental health problem, if not within their own circle of friends and family, then through a celebrity or sportsperson publicising their personal problems.

The term 'mental health disorders' covers a wide spectrum, but I wish that the term 'emotional health problems' could be recognised and used instead in many cases. Here, I am not including genetic disorders, or people with brain damage: a great many people given a 'mental health disorders' label in fact have problems controlling their emotions, and the root to their emotional distress lies in childhood. Unfortunately, many emotional health problems have become medicalised and medicated, with varying degrees of success and sometimes a multitude of associated problems. Here are some examples.

Depression

There is an accepted belief that depression arises from a chemical imbalance in the brain, especially in the levels of a chemical called serotonin. The pharmaceutical cure suggested is chemical and provided by anti-depressants. There is some truth in the chemical imbalance in the brain, but our everyday actions can bring a change in the balance of serotonin, such as laughing, exercise, lovemaking, gardening or listening to music. Correct nutrition has its part to play too, and the role of good quality sleep is crucial.

Anxiety disorders

The pharmaceutical solution to anxiety disorders often has withdrawal effects that can cause further feelings of anxiety, thus convincing a person that they still have the problem. Simple breathing exercises can bring about immediate changes to the nervous system. That the mind and body cannot be calm and anxious at the same time is a fact. An excess of caffeine and other stimulants can cause symptoms of anxiety too.

Cognitive-behavioural therapy

GPs often prescribe cognitive behavioural therapy (CBT) for help with emotional problems. Problems can occur if one is thinking and behaving in an unhelpful manner. CBT can help someone change their thoughts and behaviours to more useful and healthy ones. There are a variety of ways to help someone achieve this. A warning should be sounded about prolonged therapeutic interventions, which may lead to some emotional wounds becoming toxic. Ensuring a person's emotional needs are being met healthily, or met at all, can have successful outcomes, as can addressing the misuse of natural abilities, such as the imagination – often in a short space of time.

The consequences of not having emotional needs met as a child can result in the adult searching through their life to find these unmet needs. In observing behaviours and using these needs as a compass, I suggest that often, the missing needs of childhood are being looked for decades later. The adult may be observed behaving like 'a needy child'. That's because they were – then. In the present day, there are times when that 'needy child' can hijack the adult.

In Yorkshire, teacher and head of department, Felicity Davis's autobiography, *Guard a Silver Sixpence*, she explains that an abusive upbringing led to her emotional needs not being met. She eventually realised that she was sabotaging loving, adult relationships by being "too needy":

> I became dimly aware that I had been a very needy girlfriend indeed, and I had scared him. I had gone round to his house at almost every opportunity because it was so much more wonderful than being in my own home, and I was besotted with him and besotted with the whole business of feeling loved after so long feeling so very unloved.

> It was not surprising that in the end Dave found me far too intense, too needy – emotionally greedy would be more accurate – and felt like he needed some air. I was just impossible to be around for any length of time.

Some questions to consider

Q: What enables some people who have been given a chronic or terminal diagnosis to enjoy a quality of life, while others deteriorate?

Q: When do people who say "I have everything I want" experience a lack of fulfilment?

Q: Why do some lottery winners increase their happiness with their winnings, while others claim: "The lottery ruined my life"?

Q: How do some people find the ability to pick themselves up after a major knock back, while others do not, or find it difficult?

The answers do not just lie in positive thinking or being lucky – they come later. If a person has their emotional needs met, they are more likely to be able to cope with any life events and personal challenges. The fewer needs that are met, the more difficult it will be. This could be seen after the London bombings of July 2005: hundreds of people were affected and traumatised. Many of the people involved were young, working men and women living away from home, strangers in their neighbourhood and without a support network of friends and family nearby. They found recovery more difficult.

What does it mean to thrive?

A definition of thriving is to grow healthily and vigorously: to get on, to do well, to be successful, flourish and prosper; to blossom, to bloom. Any living organism will survive and thrive in its environment only if it has its needs met. Humans who get their fundamental emotional and physical needs met in healthy ways are more likely to thrive in life. Neglect of this side of life can lead to unhappiness and emotional health disorders.

What are these personal needs, and how do they differ from wants? For example, a newborn baby's immediate needs are the basic ones of food, warmth and sleep – without these, the baby will die. At any age, deprivation of those basic needs eventually will cause death. Moreover, the baby needs to feel a sense of physical security, whether held close to another person or wrapped up securely.

Attachment between the baby and another person starts immediately, with attention being given and sought.

If the baby is deprived of any of these basic needs in the first few weeks of life it will show physical signs called 'failure to thrive'. The baby may be lethargic, their skin will lack tone; it may cry or whimper, if it has the energy. The baby may lose its sucking reflex. It will lose weight and without intervention, death will follow.

As the baby grows, its needs increase. Toys are introduced to stretch the baby's physical abilities of movement and to stimulate the senses. Verbal and non-verbal communication increase, and the baby starts to smile and laugh. Familiar faces and voices will be recognised. Different foods are introduced, with nutrients to encourage muscle, bone and cell growth. The baby recognises routine, and there is a meaning and purpose to their waking hours: a time for food, play and sleep.

As the months and years go by, so a child's needs increase. Social interaction becomes important: they enjoy fun and friendship. They learn to give attention as well as receiving it. Learning new skills is continuous, exercise is encouraged. They feel special to someone, and love and are loved. They begin to recognise their position in the family and the wider world.

During all this time, parents, teachers and carers have been in control of meeting the child's needs. The child has very little choice: they do not recognise the difference between what they need and what they want. They will think and say that they need something when they really only want it. Parents and carers can make the mistake of giving their children what they want at the loss of what they need. Often, material goods will replace emotional contact: another example of short-term gain, but long-term pain.

Mick Brookes, former general secretary of the National Association of Head Teachers, spoke at the union's 2006 conference in Harrogate. He suggested that youngsters are subject to "loving neglect" by parents who "love their children too much to say no".

As the child matures, so they start to be able to take control over increasing areas of their lives: they learn that they can make choices. They learn how to solve problems. They can imagine solutions. Children also learn how to cope with frustrations, failure, fear, loss and provocation: these are a part of life, and learning how to control emotional reactions is part of a mature response to difficulties. They learn to draw their own boundaries and show self-discipline. Except in so many cases, adults are unable to control their emotional reactions; their words and actions regress to a child state. Maybe it is just for a minute or two, perhaps for hours, but sometimes it is for days, weeks and in severe cases, even for years. It may not be obvious what the adult is feeling and thinking, but their behaviour is revealing.

As stated, if a baby is failing to thrive it will show distress physically. A child's physical and emotional distress will show in wider behaviour problems:

- attention-seeking behaviour
- the use of old comforting behaviours
- outbursts of emotion – crying or temper
- irritation
- lying
- sulking
- hitting
- biting
- throwing
- sleep problems
- complaining of feeling unwell – whether real or imagined

- bed-wetting
- head-banging and other self-harming actions
- eating problems
- not wanting to go to school or go out to play

Most of that list also could apply to adults experiencing emotional and mental health problems. The problems will arise from:

1. adult needs not being met at all, or in an unhealthy way;

2. adults trying to meet unmet childhood needs, which always will be as elusive as the end of the rainbow; or

3. adult needs met in ways that childhood needs were met.

Returning to the original questions:

Q: What enables some people who have been given a chronic or terminal diagnosis to enjoy a quality of life, while others quickly deteriorate?

A: People who have their emotional needs met will be better able to manage their situation. Those who don't, will not.

Q: When do people who say "I have everything I want" experience a lack of fulfilment?

A: When they are surrounded by material wealth, but not emotional well-being.

Q: Why do some lottery winners increase their happiness with their winnings, while others claim: "The lottery ruined my life"?

A: The unhappy winners will have a richness of material wealth, but not a richness in friends, life's purpose and friendships.

Q: How do some people find the ability to pick themselves up after a major knock back, while others do not, or find it difficult?

A: Those that do not will feel out of control. They often concentrate on what they cannot do with what they don't have, instead of focusing on what they can do with what they do have.

In February 2010 I was watching a news report about the then British Prime Minister, Gordon Brown, who was making an official apology to child migrants. These were children who had been taken from England to Australia between 1930 and 1970 as part of the 'Child Migration to Australia' scheme. The reason was for a supposedly better life than the one they were experiencing in the UK, but in the majority of cases it led to a life of abuse, neglect and abandonment. One woman, aged between 50 and 60, was interviewed. She was extremely distressed, and despaired at not having enough money to come to the UK and meet her family. With tears streaming down her face, she exclaimed that she just wanted to know that she belonged, and was loved.

My tears flowed too. I immediately thought of the aforementioned list of emotional needs we need to have met, not only in order to survive in life, but to thrive. As a child, the Australian woman and so many thousands of other children had not had their emotional needs met, and in that adult woman's voice I heard a child crying for help to get her missing needs met – to belong, and to be loved. I went to bed and reprimanded myself for watching the news before bedtime, being something I had stopped doing to get a better night's sleep. I lay in bed and tossed and turned for more than two hours: old memories had been triggered, and I couldn't get the images out of my head.

In the late 1960s I trained as a nursery nurse in a children's home for the under-fives in Windsor, Berkshire. It was a respectable place and very well run by the Church of England Children's Society. There was one babies section in the home, and two toddler and children's sections, with some 30 to 40 children in total. The children were well cared for and I have plenty of photos of smiling, well-dressed and clean boys and girls. The trainee nursery nurses were loving and caring. Over 40 years I have often wondered what happened to the children, but until watching that TV programme I had never really given any thought to the fact that those children spent the first five years of their life having some of their fundamental needs unmet. The staff changed every few months, as we moved around during the training, and we were all dressed in nurse's uniforms. Also, there were very few men around. The odds are that some of the children will be drawn to uniforms in getting their adult intimate needs met, and they will not know why. Many will be trying desperately to get their unmet childhood needs met, but failing over and over again.

More memories flooded my mind. I was taken back to the early 1950s. My mother had to go away with my grandmother while my sister and I were left in a residential nursery, Norlands, in Chislehurst, Kent. I stayed when I was two and three years old, just for a few days each visit. Even though I was so young, I still hold a few images of playing in the garden, seeing a nurse with my baby sister and walking in a crocodile line, but don't remember anything unpleasant happening at all. Neither do I think I have repressed anything, but would I know? What I do know is that I didn't like watching through the window as my mother walked away. Years later, at 17 years old, I steadfastly refused even to entertain going to Norlands for nursery nurse training, and even now I still experience a frisson of totally irrational dislike if I hear the name 'Chislehurst'. I wonder if deeply rooted emotional reactions could explain 'a sixth sense', a 'gut' feeling?

If that was my reaction, I cannot help but wonder how many of the children from the Windsor home have been able to grow up emotionally after their experiences. They may have succeeded in different fields, but how many may still be searching for what doesn't exist? Was I looking for something when I chose childcare as an occupation? As for the Australians, even if they do manage to get over to the UK and meet family, they will never get their childhood back. Perhaps this is an obvious thing to say, but too many people try to do exactly that and wonder why they feel so let down and disappointed afterwards.

This experience could be repeated with children who were evacuees in the Second World War. In modern psychological language, this would be described as an attachment disorder, but I suggest that the root is a childhood feeling of fear that is hijacking the adult, and could be outgrown. Not all people who have been abandoned in their childhood are emotionally unwell.

Personal experience

I walked into a clothes shop. I saw a skirt on a rail and liked it immediately – this is unusual in itself. I admired it, held it and imagined wearing it. The price was okay, but I knew that it was an expense I could do without. The emotional pull was almost physical. I stepped away, but with a "Go on, you deserve it" voice shouting in one ear. The quieter, "This may not be a good idea" voice was being drowned out.

I thought about the clothes already at home in the cupboard. I thought about the credit card bill that would arrive in a month, and said to myself, "Do I really need this skirt, or just want it?"

The answer was simple. I went back to the skirt: it had become an overpriced piece of coloured cloth that I certainly didn't need. I walked out of the shop without the skirt: a victory to the small, quiet voice of calm.

I am not going to pretend that this technique works every time, especially if it is chocolate at any time, or an alcoholic drink around 6pm. Sometimes the loud wanting voice will win. However, give it a try next time you find yourself convinced that you "really really need" it. Making a break between thinking and doing works well too: it uses the brain's natural rhythms. Twenty minutes is considered a reasonable time, although switching the brain hemispheres from emotional to logical thinking need only take 30 seconds. After a break, the "I need it, I must have it" coming from the emotional brain is replaced by "I just want it and can go without it" from the rational and logical brain.

Illustration

Here are two news stories from different ends of the spectrum, with similarities and a personal interest.

1. A ten-year-old boy, Harry Hucknall, was described as "a bit naughty, a bit overactive and didn't do as he was told". He was diagnosed with attention deficit hyperactivity disorder (ADHD) and depression. He was prescribed with Ritalin and Prozac.

He hanged himself.

2. A man called Bear Grylls tells of himself as a seven-year-old in his autobiography, Mud, Sweat and Tears. He was naughty, overactive and did not do as he was told.

He is now an international adventurer, author, TV personality and the UK's Chief Scout of the Scouting Association.

The first case, of Harry Hucknall, is tragic, although this story is not unique, either with children or adults. Any internet search will reveal many concerning cases of lives lost while on medication that may or may not be working.

Both sounded like lively boys with lively minds and bodies. Minds and bodies that needed to be loved, stretched, given attention, exercised, listened to and encouraged. There also needed to be recognition and encouragement of their own particular skills and interests, even if no adult quite understood them.

One boy was medicated.
The other boy was educated.
One boy died.
The other boy thrived.
One boy is a cautionary tale.
The other boy has tales to tell.

Reflection

Make a list of:

- Four recent clothing purchases.

- Six recent non-food or drink purchases.

- Six recent snacks or meals you have eaten.

- Six recent drinks you have consumed.

Think about each one. Did you want or need it? Did you decide not to have it, but then justified changing your mind?

Can you name the emotion behind making your decision?

Did the feelings of pleasure of having it dissipate a few minutes or hours later?

Next time you feel a strong emotional pull to eat, drink or buy something, try this: say to yourself, "Do I need it or just want it?"

You may be able to justify very easily that you do, definitely need it – but do you really?

Stop, take a few deep, slow breaths, and think about what could happen next. It need only take 20 to 30 seconds for the brain to switch hemispheres, but a bit longer can be more helpful.

I was in a church one day, when I saw this list pinned to a board:

I asked for strength and I was given difficulties to make me strong.

I asked for wisdom and I was given problems to learn to solve.

I asked for prosperity and I was given brain and brawn to work.

I asked for courage and I was given dangers to overcome.

I asked for love and I was given troubled people to help.

I asked for favours and I was given opportunities.

I received nothing I wanted.

I received everything I needed.

Chapter 2

'I don't know how to do it': abilities, skills and talents

Failure is success if we learn from it.

Malcolm Forbes

❛❛What on earth are transferable skills?", said the frustrated woman in front of me. Christine had been asked this question at a job interview and had no idea how to answer it. We went through some of the jobs that she had to do at home and her hobbies and pastimes, naming the various skills that she needed to complete and enjoy the tasks. Then we went through all the skills that she had picked up at school, college and her workplace. Now she had a list of transferable skills. These were skills that she had learned over a period of time. Nature has given us transferable skills too.

Parts of the brain

Different parts of the brain have different functions.

Memory

This can be a double-edged sword. Memories can range from being blissful to nightmares. Memories are tagged in the brain with emotions and triggered by any of our senses: there can be a full range of reactions, from barely there to very strong and debilitating. A smell, sight, sound, taste or touch can whizz the brain backwards in time in a nanosecond: far quicker time travel than anything Dr Who can invent. The downside is that the memory can play tricks, and we do not always remember it exactly how it was, although we are often absolutely sure that we do. Each person's experiences are informed by their unique memory-matches and associated emotions, which is why siblings who experience the same life event, can hold such different memories about it. Police taking witness statements know they will get as many different viewpoints as people.

Positive memories help us grow and learn. We can use the memories of how we did something, travelled somewhere or made something in the past to help us in the present. Negative memories can be learning experiences too.

"I remember when I did this and it worked well."
"I remember when I did this and it didn't work well."

Problem-solving

Because of memory-matches, we can solve problems. However, if we are too emotional it can become difficult, because emotional arousal narrows the access to the logical brain – then we may do something illogical because we cannot think properly. This is one reason why a therapy session full of emotion is not the best way to find solutions to the problems being aired.

Separate brain hemispheres

The emotional brain and the logical brain are in different parts of the brain. They can work well on their own in the appropriate context, or in balance (see Appendix 1).

Example

Reading a book, listening to music or watching a film can involve the emotional brain being in charge, with little need for the logical brain to work. Reading instructions, making a presentation or looking at a timetable needs the logical brain to take charge. Any emotional arousal is unhelpful and can lead to mistakes being made. It is amazing how plain English can appear like gobbledegook if the brain is emotionally aroused: for example, if one is running late, looking at a departure board at a station or airport and attempting to make sense of it can be challenging. Mistakes can be made. The same can happen when giving presentations.

Imagination and creativity

Again, this is a double-edged sword. Creativity takes imagination; so do anxiety and depressive disorders, which involve misuse of the imagination.

Self-observation

This is an internal 'CCTV camera' to help with self-awareness, and an often underused resource.

Communication

We can convey our wants, needs and fears by both verbal and non-verbal communication. For example:

Client: "My wife doesn't communicate with me. In bed, she just turns her back on me."

Me: "I'd say she was communicating with you quite loudly with her body language."

Client [bursting into tears]: "My wife has been talking to me for years."

A mind–body connection

It is of concern that there are still a few doctors and scientists around who do not believe that there is a connection between the mind and body. I can understand that when faced with a set of physical symptoms, it must be easier to match the symptoms to a physical cause, but I suspect the role that the mind can have in some illnesses will always cause debate. The reverse is true too. As a GP friend, Dan, told me when I challenged him, "We can only guesstimate." Perhaps it is easier to medicate the body rather than understand the mind?

Personal experience

In 2010, for insurance purposes, I had to undergo a set of thorough and expensive tests. In fear of the small print, I had declared a health incident that I was pretty sure was to do with the stress of a terminally-ill parent, a house sale and house renovation. The results were inconclusive. One consultant told me to take some strong medication "just in case". Another told me: "As a therapist I'm surprised to see you here. I'd have thought you'd have treated yourself." I chose the latter course of action.

1. The brain memory-matches through the five senses: sight, sound, hearing, touch and taste.

A sensory trigger leads to a memory-match, which leads to an emotional reaction, leading to a thought and behaviour.

2. Emotional arousal can increase 'stupidity'.

I heard these words at my first seminar on my psychotherapy diploma course in 1998. I flinched. How dare anyone call me 'stupid', although I had absorbed those beliefs from childhood. The tutor went on to explain and I listened intently. It made sense. It still makes sense. So I use the word deliberately: 'stupid' is an emotive word, but if you think about behaviours that can occur from being highly emotional, I think most of us would admit to having been 'stupid' at times.

Arousal occurs in the right brain hemisphere and, as it rises, it prevents the left brain from working properly, where logic and rational thinking occur. You cannot think straight, and sometimes this can lead to behaving in illogical, irrational or 'stupid' ways: for example, by panicking or embarrassing yourself. Emotional arousal can be lowered by different methods: slowing down breathing, exercise, mind diversion and distraction (see Appendix 3).

3. The nervous system has evolved so that the body cannot be anxious and calm at the same time: a simple but helpful truth.

4. The mind's internal dialogue influences the quality-of-life experience.

Thoughts influence actions and beliefs. If the thoughts are not helpful, they can be changed. Beliefs can switch capabilities on or off – they can be changed. Small changes can make a big difference.

5. Attention versus neglect.

The more attention given to a behaviour or thought pattern, the stronger it becomes; the less attention, the weaker it gets.

6. Behaviour patterns.

It takes around six weeks for a new pattern of behaviour to become a habit, depending on frequency of repetition: for example, learning a language or dance step. Concentrated learning shortens the time needed. Basic personalities do not change, unless there is brain damage or mind-altering substances are involved, but responses can be changed.

Female and male differences

In the same way that the word 'stupid' can cause debate, so can the topic of 'the gendered brain'. I support equality of the sexes, but have felt uneasy at times about some of the stronger aims of feminism. I have witnessed women walking out of seminars when this subject is being discussed, refusing to believe that there could be a male brain/female brain.

I was taking a workshop with mental health professionals; at times I use humour to make a challenging point. I was talking about the gendered brain. One of the female participants was heavily pregnant. She challenged me strongly: "Are you telling us that men and women think differently?" I responded by saying, "Yes, and I believe you are about to find out how." The mood lifted.

From Brainsex:

> The brain, like a body, has a sex.
>
> Brainsex

How we become male or female in physical appearance is well understood. We have 46 chromosomes: 22 of these are pairs, and look the same in both the male and female. The sex chromosomes are the key: the male is XY, and the female XX. At six weeks the foetus is sex-neutral.

In normal development the male foetus produces male hormones, including testosterone. The process is triggered by the male's Y chromosome. The hormones activate a cascade of genes that code for maleness. Without this, the foetus becomes female.

Hormones are all powerful – a genetic XY male, deprived of male hormones, will develop female physical characteristics. A genetic XX female, exposed to male hormones, will develop male physical characteristics.

These same hormones also influence human behaviour. The male foetus in the womb is exposed to five times more male hormones than the female.

Ann Moir
(co-author of *Brainsex: The Real Difference Between Men and Women*, with kind permission)

Free will and choice

The majority of people have free will and choice: this is not a terribly popular concept when a person does not want to take responsibility for their actions, but ultimately it is true.

You can live life or relive life, but you cannot do both. You cannot change the past, only your attitude to it. Generally, there are only two ways of dealing with any problem or personal crisis:

1. Finding a solution to the problem.

2. Adapting our thoughts and behaviour to manage a life event.

Looking for a third or fourth option may delay putting options 1 and 2 into practice, leading to further emotional distress.

Learning how to learn

Often, clients have looked incredulous when I pointed out to even the most intelligent that they have spent their formative lives failing at everything they tried: whether it was walking, talking, writing, reading, getting dressed or feeding themselves. Their carers would, in the main, have encouraged them to try and try again, giving praise for the tiniest success. Then somewhere it can change: the praise turns into "What's the matter with you, are you stupid?" – and the message is received. To not get something right is wrong, and brings with it uncomfortable feelings; maybe lack of attention, or a withdrawal of love. Perhaps it is physical punishment or, just as damaging to a young brain, public humiliation.

We may give up trying altogether, or try extra hard. Or we may just plod on through life, but with a panicky feeling that is switched on any time we have to learn something new. If we can get out of doing something, we will: for example, learning computer skills. I am surprised that in 2013 there are adults who still avoid learning new technology, which has become a necessity in everyday life. And is not just older members of the community either. Sometimes, the mental torture we put ourselves through is worth the effort, such as driving lessons. The brain has to make new neurological connections for new skills, because nothing already exists – although there could be something similar, but not quite the same.

Imagine you are leading a group of people through a woodland walk, and you come across a blocked path. Going back is not an option, so you have to find a new way forward – the others are relying on you. To the left and right you are surrounded by a mass of thick undergrowth, with no obvious path; you have to hack your way through. It takes effort and persistence. You want to give up, but you don't. The person behind is treading the undergrowth down, and each person behind is doing the same. By the time it comes to the last person in the group, their way through is easy.

The brain is no different. Practice, and lots of it, will lay down new pathways and create new helpful habits. If woodland walking isn't for you, then remember one of the following: when you have changed your furniture around at home; when the layout of the supermarket has changed (as they always do); when a part of your body has been out of action; or when the software on your computer upgraded – in fact, anything where you have had to temporarily stop a habitual behaviour and consciously learn something new. It felt awkward at first, but then you adapt – the brain adapts.

All learning follows the same rules, whether it is a new job, language, way of thinking or hobby. Generally, the initial learning does not come easily – why should it? We need to make strong neurological connections in the brain in order for the brain to work properly. However, I should point out that I do not find the message 'Practice makes perfect' helpful. 'Practice can make better' may be a more helpful phrase.

What messages do you hear as you are learning new ways? Messages that come from the long and distant past and belong to others? That you are hopeless, stupid, a failure? If, so why are you still listening? Together with laying down new software, we also have to battle with the ghostly emotional voices from the past telling us that we cannot do it. If these voices are allowed to take over our emotional brain, then our natural intelligence can be temporarily put on hold until we become calmer and can think clearly again.

Sarah was attending an evening class. The tutor came up to see how she was doing. "It's awful,", she said, "I just can't do this." The tutor replied, "Yes, and that's why you're here."

Much has been written about a human being becoming proficient, even an expert, after approximately 10,000 hours. While this has been shown to be generally true, it does not take into account innate talent. For example, I am not a natural linguist, musician or artist, but I know that being immersed in a language, a creative activity or practising an instrument for hours, eventually I would become proficient (although it would be tough going). Some of my family are natural linguists, musicians and artists and have an innate talent: it would take them fewer than 10,000 hours to become expert.

We all possess innate talents, but often they stay hidden and undiscovered. Schools do not always bring out these talents and skills, and thousands of teenagers finish their education believing that they are fairly useless, when actually their non-academic natural skills and talents were never discovered or encouraged. The education system in the UK for the majority of children does not appear to give enough credence to natural talents. The focus seems to be on testing and grading natural talents off the educational radar. Cities, towns and villages all have people who have been 'written off', who say that they are stupid, but are not.

Personal experience

When I was 42, I had an annual staff appraisal. Some extremely positive managerial skills were mentioned. I was astonished. They were just behaviours that I did naturally, and they were not anything in which I could have taken an exam. How different my life could have been if these skills had been recognised when I was a teenager.

When I moved to a new part of the country, I answered an advertisement in the local paper, and a few weeks later was chosen to be part of a chocolate tasting panel. It turns out that I have excellent sensory talents. Just think where that might have taken me from school, had it been known then? However, excellence in my school was judged on exam success, so I, and many friends, left believing that we were 'stupid', which was far from the truth.

Adversity can bring out hidden talents. The recession has caused difficulties for many people: some people who have had to rely on themselves more have discovered that they are capable of doing all kinds of things. I do not recommend war, but the First and Second World Wars showed women that they could do so much more than housework or office duties.

Moreover, these talents do not have to be creative ones. In 2011, I was in a branch of a leading supermarket. A floor manager opened a folder of papers in front of me, including a mathematical matrix for meal break entitlements: it looked a well-used piece of paper. I couldn't help but mention that I had designed it, and told them the story of its inception. "Was it difficult to do?", someone asked. "No," I replied. "It just came to me in a meeting."

I was considered so poor at maths at school that I was not allowed to sit any maths exams. Yet I designed the matrix in 1993, and in 2011 the store manager told me, "It has not been improved by modern technology." At the time I was given a £100 bonus for 'a good idea', but not before someone from head office had come to the shop to check that the design really was the work of the lowly checkout manager using her own innate talents: something that a whole department in head office had not been able to do.

In therapy, it is important to discover a person's abilities and skills to help them problem-solve. It is these abilities and skills that can be turned to their advantage and help them find a way out of the difficulties they find themselves experiencing. It was one of my favourite parts of being a therapist. It was like opening a box of treasure. There were always nuggets of gold and some precious jewels.

Most people seeking therapy think that they are not good enough in some way. If they are occupied in their day-to-day life doing something that isn't a particular talent, then it is not going to help their overall confidence. Doing something that comes from deep within and feels natural may help. This does not mean that it has to be easy, because we also gain confidence from meeting a challenge.

Illustration

I loved a TV programme called *Hidden Talents* on Channel 4. What a brilliant idea: finding people with hidden talents, and giving them a chance to develop them – an idea, given unlimited finances, I would love to roll out nationwide, especially with young people, who so often arrive at the end of education with undiscovered skills and talents believing that they are a failure.

The programme's presenter, Richard Bacon, said on his radio show:

"Most professional footballers are already showing their skills at the age of eight. What about the children who don't have the opportunity to show what they can do? Who knows what they could achieve?"

Exactly.

Arthur and Joan took an unexpected chance to move to a small town in Dorset. They were in their early eighties when they swapped their London flat for a Dorset bungalow. They were thrilled to get out of the city: they embraced life in the town, and took interest in some of the local classes on offer at the local community hall, one of which was painting. Due to basic schooling, the war years and working life, neither of them had taken art classes before. They thought that they would give it a try. Arthur discovered a hidden talent: he could paint watercolours and, before he died, he was showing them at local exhibitions.

Reflection

After a long, colder and wetter than usual spring, I was glorying one morning in the sight of blue sky, sunshine and snowdrops. I was reminded of how much there is in nature that provides us with the lessons of life and innate talents and skills – if we want to learn from them. Here are a few thoughts arising from the view from my study window.

Snowdrops

Snowdrops are one of the most fragile flowers in the plant world. It is so easy to crush the stem, even with careful handling, yet they come through the earth when it is at its hardest and coldest – they thrive in those conditions. A fresh dumping of snow can arrive, disrupting people's lives, yet the snowdrop still survives.

Clouds

The sun is always in the sky during daylight; it is just that sometimes cloud hides it. Taking off from an airport in the pouring rain and going up through the clouds never fails to lift my spirits.

Seeds

Seeds can be dried up, wrinkled and look worthy of throwing away – but given the right conditions of water, warmth and suitable environment, they should thrive, blossom and be fruitful.

Weeds

There can be beauty and nourishment in plants that we call weeds.

Seasons

From the Bible, Ecclesiastes 3:1–8:

1. To every thing there is a season, and a time to every purpose under the heavens;

2. A time to be born, and a time to die; a time to plant, a time to reap that which is planted;

3. A time to kill, and a time to heal; a time to break down, and a time to build up;

4. A time to weep, and a time to laugh; a time to mourn, and a time to dance;

5. A time to cast away stones, and a time to gather stones together; a time to embrace, and a time to refrain from embracing;

6. A time to get, and a time to lose; a time to keep, and a time to cast away;

7. A time to rend, and a time to sew; a time to keep silence, and a time to speak;

8. A time to love, and a time to hate; a time of war, and a time of peace.

Butterflies

Butterflies need to go through the struggle of pushing themselves through a cocoon to fly. It is the struggle that gives them life.

Sights and sounds

We look, but may not see. We hear, but may not listen.

Birds

I remember a woman I met once in a lift. For no particular reason she said, "Aren't birds wonderful? It doesn't matter what happens to them in life, they always start the next day singing."

It is worth thinking about.

Chapter 3

'I want it – now!': instant gratification

> *All human errors are impatience, a premature breaking off of methodical procedure, an apparent fencing-in of what is apparently at issue.*
>
> **Franz Kafka**

In the 1970s, credit cards were introduced by the banks. The slogan on one advertisement for the Access card was "Takes the waiting out of wanting". Very tempting it was too. People could walk into a shop and buy something, even if they did not have the money. There had always been credit: it was called hire purchase, but this was slightly different. This was instant. No forms to fill in, just a piece of plastic to hand over.

As children we have an undeveloped concept of time. Most of us will talk of endless summers, but they seem to pass in a flash these days. A school term seemed to last forever, let alone a school year, which felt like a lifetime.

Speaking about one day, three days, even seven days to a small child is generally useless. A newer concept of understanding comes with 'X many sleeps': a child's brain can manage processing the thought of having to go to bed and being asleep, as it tends to happen in a routine way, in the same place – but days? With their infinite variety of people and places to confuse the brain? Unlikely, but we would not talk to an adult about something happening in so many 'sleeps'.

Adults say "in a minute" to a child's request for attention: that minute can last a very long time. A child soon learns not to trust that anything will happen "in a minute". While new technology brings us many benefits, we are losing the ability to wait.

How much has modern technology got to do with an increase in anger problems, relating to not getting what one wants – now! As an adult in the twenty-first century, we expect a great deal of instant gratification. Modern technology has provided us with a myriad of equipment that is fun to use and provides instant results, but the experience of going without or waiting for something, and the ability to do so, are declining with alarming consequences:

- mobile phones
- social media
- 24-hour news
- the internet
- credit cards
- mp3 players
- fast food

I embrace new technology and enjoy the instant gratification it offers. However, it does not encourage the ability to learn self-control, or the use of self-discipline. It is not just with technology that instant gratification can lead to problems. Addictive behaviour arises from the inability to control powerful urges to "want it and want it now." When such adults try to bring up their own children, it is not easy – this is why, on childrearing and parenting TV programmes, it is the parents who have to change and then the child will change, not the other way round.

Here are some comparative examples of child and adult attitudes. We should all be able to identify with them.

- The child wants what they cannot have; the adult can go without.
- The child wants it now; the adult can wait.
- The child can give up easily; the adult can problem-solve.
- The child wants others to do it for them; adults can do it themselves.
- The child says "It's not fair"; the adult says "Life isn't".
- The child blames others; the adult takes responsibility.
- The child is dependent on others; the adult likes doing things themselves.
- The child acts firsts and thinks afterwards; the adult can think before acting.
- The child is a dependant; the adult can be independent.
- The child is self-centred; adults look outside their own ego.

I am sure there are others, but I have left one more until last. This one plays an enormous part in whether the adult can shake off the shackles of the child:

- The child believes what others say about them; the adult can make up their own mind.

A common example of observing adults wanting instant gratification is watching a colleague throw a tantrum in a meeting. Moments when you and your colleagues may want to shout, "Oh for God's sake, grow up!" There is the clue. The adult is temporarily behaving like a child. They may not physically look like a child, except perhaps in their mannerisms. They may not dress like a child, or even show the intelligence of a child, but they are becoming like a child emotionally.

Tantrums and tiaras

Discussing the subject of this book with a variety of people has elicited some great responses. People would sometimes recognise the behaviours in their families, but more so in their workplaces.

1. Peter wasn't getting his own way in a discussion in a board meeting. He shouted and stomped out of the room. He did this regularly; his boss was never really able to manage him properly, and tended to give in to him.

2. Lucy's temper exploded in the office because the work was not going the way that she felt it ought to go. She could not tolerate anything less than perfection.

3. Alison felt that she was being left out of a discussion in a management meeting. She got up from the table dramatically and went out of the room, slamming the door behind her.

4. Colin was quietly disruptive when someone was presenting or speaking.

Yes, I am embarrassed to admit that I am No. 3.

It can be embarrassing to watch an adult throw a tantrum, and I am sure that most of us have experienced this at some point. I will run through the examples given and suggest some possible triggers for the action.

1. Peter, in his fifties, was an only child and close to his mother, who idolised him. He held a prestigious academic position in a university. He regularly had tantrums in the workplace, generally shouting, screaming, banging the table and walking out of meetings. Most of the time he succeeded in getting his own way.

I would suggest that while he had a high IQ, his EQ (emotional intelligence) did not match: he presented as a man/boy. He had grown up getting his own way by having tantrums, and was indulged by staff members. Unless someone was able to draw boundaries and be consistent in their non-acceptance of his behaviour, it was likely to continue.

2. This is a common problem. Lucy had a high IQ and a long list of achievements. She also had a feeling of not being good enough, carried from childhood experiences. For every document she produced, there had been ten, twenty, thirty drafts. She can never be satisfied with her work.

My suggestion for this behaviour is that while this kind of person's IQ is high and their adult achievements testify to this fact, they are driven by childhood experiences of their work not being considered good enough. This could have come from a teacher or family member. It may be a perception rather than an actual event, but their EQ in delivering work is stuck in childhood.

When I did my training, I was taught that "perfectionists achieve nothing". That is not quite true, but they probably dispose of some really excellent work and ideas on the way to producing the final piece of work. Productivity is lower than need be, and time-wasting can add to the stress of deadlines.

People with perfectionist tendencies often have high levels of anxiety. It is not good for general health to have stress hormones such as cortisol and noradrenaline coursing through the body all the time – they are wonderful in small doses, but can damage the body in a variety of ways if allowed to flow constantly.

3. I remember this well, though it was 30 years ago. I behaved in a sulky way, wound myself up and made a dramatic exit. Why? Because I didn't feel I was being included. Someone had forgotten to inform me of the meeting. I felt ignored and left out. Not good enough. It wasn't fair! I resorted to an attention-seeking behaviour: it worked in so much as I drew attention to myself, but my colleagues were not impressed. Fortunately I was not indulged, and never did it again – there were more adult ways to communicate. I know I was resorting to mini-me who wasn't listened to nor opinions acknowledged,

but that was then, and this was now. I needed to 'grow up' – so I did.

4. A person is part of a group listening to a speaker or watching a presentation. The subject may be of little interest to them, it may be boring, it may be being poorly delivered: we have all been in meetings like that. The person quietly, but noticeably, shows their dissatisfaction. They feel they are superior in some way to the speaker. They start to engage a neighbour in low-level asides or pass notes, just like being in the back row at school.

Reliving the past

So many people buy their children material things, social standing and education because "I never had it". If it is bought with their child's needs in mind, then the outcome may be better than if these things were really bought to replace the adult's own missing childhood need. No child can relive their parent's upbringing, and it can cause a great amount of unhappiness all round if tried – whether it is clothing, toys, education, sporting or artistic activities, or personal relationships. (A good book on adults living out their dreams unwisely through their children is *The Available Parent: Radical Optimism for Raising Teens and Tweens* by John Duffy; see Bibliography.)

Personal experience

When I was about ten years old, the latest summer craze was hoola hoops. Not the potato crisp, but a large ring of bright plastic, which young girls spent hours spinning around their waist. I loved the ones my friends had and wanted one of my own. I only had presents at Christmas and birthdays. The hoola hoop was considered a toy, and a toy was a present. My birthday is in May, which had passed, so I had to wait.

Christmas morning dawned, and there at the end of my bed was a bright blue hoola hoop. I was happy, but not as much as I might have been. In fact, just writing about it can bring back memories of childhood disappointment. Why? The fad had passed. The moment had gone. I played with it a lot, but not with any thrill.

I have seen them in the shops over the years as they come in and out of fashion, but would not dream of buying one to capture a lost childhood moment. That was then; this is now.

There is nothing wrong with buying things to capture youthful memories, as long as we do not expect to relive those times exactly. The problems arise from the delusion that can arise when we expect that reliving the memory will be just like it was the first time. It won't be and leads to thwarted expectations. A mature emotional brain will recognise that; an immature emotional brain will keep on trying.

Example

I was explaining these behaviours to my husband, Alex. Due to his mother's acute anxiety problems, the children were not allowed to own or ride a bike, or learn to swim. As an adult, Alex learned to swim and bought a bike. Over the following years he cycled all over Europe without coming to any harm. I explained that if he had behaved in an emotional way, and let the deprived mini-me take over his decision-making, he would have kept on buying new bikes in the hope of providing his 'mini-me' with his missing need – but he would never have been satisfied, however many bikes he bought.

Addiction is the seeking of an emotion through a physical behaviour and needing to increase the intensity to keep getting the emotion. Without the need for instant gratification there would be no addiction. One of the best descriptions I have heard of addiction was from the writer and humourist Clive James, who spoke on BBC Radio 4 of his history of smoking up to 80 a day, from the age of 11.

Illustration

Taken from Clive James, Smoking: My lost love. A *Point of View, BBC*, 3 August 2007.

Peppermints. Nicotine patches. Mini cigars. All were tried – to little success... So what finally worked?

Finally it was the Australia run that spelled the end of my smoking career. After 13 hours we arrived at Bangkok Airport and I raced for the smoking room ... I opened the door, saw all the other smokers ... I realised that I would have to smoke in the standing position... I realised I didn't have to light up. All I had to do was breathe in. It was the moment of truth.

But then, I had always known the truth. The truth is that I love smoking ... There is a book ... which teaches that ... from your second cigarette onwards does nothing for you except raise your nicotine level ... Possibly so, but in my case it also satisfied a deep longing, the memory of which lingers like lost love.

So how did I finally quit? I learned to smoke the memory. When the longing hits you, don't try to repress it. Savour it. The actual thing wouldn't be any better. In fact it wouldn't be as good, because it would last only as long as the cigarette ..., whereas the memory lasts as long as you like.

Reflection

The next time you want something now, stop and think about it for a moment.

Are you trying to capture a memory? Relive a time past, and consider the following.

- Food – are you eating a memory of comfort or family?
- Alcohol – are you drinking a memory of companionship, relaxation or feeling carefree?
- Gambling – are you spending money on retrieving a memory that is fun, exciting or innocent?
- Shopping – are you buying a memory?

If in doubt, stop and thinking about the feeling you are experiencing at that moment. It will not be a new feeling to you, although the circumstances may be new. The root of that feeling lies way back in time. If you think about it, a memory may pop into your mind. However, that was then – this is now.

Be kind to yourself. Set your own boundaries. It may be short-term pain, but ultimately long-term gain.

Chapter 4

'It's not fair!': acceptance and resilience

Life is never fair, and perhaps it is a good thing for most of us that it is not.

Oscar Wilde

Is there a child alive who hasn't uttered those words? Is there an adult who, if they have not actually uttered them, hasn't thought them? Hardly a week goes by when day-to-day plans are not upset by some unexpected incident and expectations are thwarted. If the incident is pleasant then it is easier to manage; but mostly there seem to be problems, and so often one problem piles one on top of another: "It's not fair!"

"It's not fair" is a cry that regularly can be heard coming from children's mouths, whether in a shout or a whine. Indeed, we discover in time that, as the grown-up response goes, "Life isn't fair" – but we learn to deal with the unfairness, managing it in more mature ways than stamping feet, slamming doors, throwing things, hitting people or misusing various substances. We can choose to accept or challenge the unfairness in a more mature way. Using the passion that lies behind a sense of unfairness and injustice can be a wonderful motivator of self and people, as long as the passion is not used by putting energy into an act of revenge, as such actions can end up with unforeseen and upsetting consequences. For example, I would not have retrained as a therapist if I had not been motivated by what I felt were great injustices in the care of people with mental health problems. The majority of charities only exist due to the founders experiencing a sense of injustice and doing something about it.

> *The world is a dangerous place, not because of those that do evil, but because of those who look on and do nothing.*
> **Albert Einstein**

We can think about why we find something unfair and perhaps understand where the root of our discontent really lies. "It's not fair" belongs to a child. Name the emotion and find the child attached to it, and you could experience a personal insight. It may be helpful in the future.

While I can bristle at the injustices in the world, I very rarely feel "it's not fair" these days. However, on the last couple of occasions when those words were on the tip of my tongue, a quick bit of self-analysis showed me that the feelings belonged to the ten-year-old mini-me who wanted to speak for me. Thank goodness for my training and some personal development.

Personal experience

I was faced with a head of department attempting to bully me in front of a colleague, the observer. His reputation was well known and, as the interview progressed, the ten-year-old was screaming inside my head to resort to shouting "It's not fair!"... and in the circumstances, it really wasn't fair at all. With tremendous effort, I stayed in control, knowing that to lose control would be disastrous. Afterwards and on my own, I burst into tears because the effort had drained me, but I had held it together and was proud of myself. The next day the man said to me, "We were very impressed how you held it together." Extraordinary. As a therapist working in his department, I was picking up the pieces of people who were unable to hold it together, although of course, as a person using bullying behaviour, he had unmet needs too.

The last time I found "it's not fair" meaningfully on my lips was about five years ago. The situation was most unjust, and other people agreed with me – but what were my options? Accepting something that could not be changed was the healthiest one, but it is so tough. I was angry: in fact, if I was to pick that particular memory, my thoughts would become toxic. This is not to say that if something isn't fair, we should roll over and accept it. However, sulking, having tantrums, crying and hoping that someone else will make the situation fair does not ultimately solve the problem.

Overcoming adversity

Taking time from introspecting on all the negative, even in the darkness there is light. It can even be life-saving. For the most wonderful illustration of this, read Joe Simpson's *Touching the Void* (see Bibliography). In practice, I have used Joe's experiences as illustrations for managing life's dark, lonely and unrelentingly miserable times. This man fell into a very deep, dark crevasse high up in the Andes. His friend had left him for dead. After a time, all he could see was a pinprick size of light very high up, a long way away. Light can bring hope. He knew that the light would be the only means of escape, so he slowly inched his battered and badly injured body, including a broken leg, towards the light. The light became a little larger until, many hours later, he had managed to crawl up the rocks to where there was a hole in the side of the mountain, letting in the light. He scrambled out of the hole, only to find himself on a glacier, and slid hundreds of yards downhill.

I recommend the book and the film: I think it should be shown in every school to teenagers. There are many stories of people overcoming adversity that could help the "it's not fair" mindset. Watching the athletes at the London 2012 Paralympic Games certainly made one consider how to positively manage times of adversity.

It's not fair – what to do next?

"Don't get mad, get even." So said Robert F. Kennedy. Well, revenge may seem satisfying in the short-term, but I do wonder about the long-term damage. I am not going to pretend that I haven't wasted many hours and days plotting some sort of action to get my own back for various slights I have felt over the years – but that is all it was: a waste of time and effort. Saying that, and in all honesty, perhaps the saying "Revenge is a dish best served cold" is satisfying in some way. However, it is infantile and reeks of "Ya boo sucks!" It could be more helpful and healthy to use the force of energy and imagination that anger can generate for positive action, rather than negative.

> *Anybody can become angry – that is easy, but to be angry with the right person and to the right degree and at the right time and for the right purpose, and in the right way – that is not within everybody's power and is not easy.*
>
> **Aristotle**

Use that anger wisely to change the unjust. Fight to get justice. There are thousands of unjust actions and events in this world. Some happen to us personally or our family, friends and community. Is it a matter you can do something about to improve the situation for yourself or others?

Acceptance

One day, when I was in my thirties, I was feeling particularly hard done by. I visited an elderly woman, Dorothy, who had shown me great kindness. I asked her: "How have you managed to deal with the unhappy things in your life?" She came out with one word: "Acceptance." I recall thinking, "No way!", but I have never forgotten what she said. All these years later, I now know what she meant. Now I understand the Serenity Prayer:

> Grant to us the serenity of mind to accept that which cannot be changed; courage to change that which can be changed, and wisdom to know the one from the other.

In her book *Guard a Silver Sixpence*, Felicity Davis gradually learned to accept her upbringing:

> I liked the idea of it [the book] helping to put things straight again, reminding us all of what really mattered in life instead of lingering over the mess that Elsie and Albert had made of much of their daughter's life, and of my childhood and of their own marriage. It fitted the occasion perfectly for me, especially the part about seeing through a glass darkly now, but having faith that one day it would all be made clear. As I threw my handful of dust on to Mum's coffin, I felt like I was saying goodbye to all of them – Hannah, Emily, Elsie, Marjorie. "I've done the best I can for you all," I told them. "I have tried to put things right, and now let's lay it all to rest."

There would be very little therapy and counselling required if we all had perfect parenting. Parenting was where all our emotional needs were initially met. The first line of Philip Larkin's famous poem, 'This Be The Verse', is quoted so many times as justification for a client's problems: "They fuck you up, your mum and dad."

Most people don't get further than the first line of the first verse, and in many cases, they are unable to get much further in solving their problems. After all, it is easy to blame others and say that life is unfair. Acceptance and wisdom comes from the second verse: "But they were fucked up in their turn." It gives perspective, and can help people understand instead of blame.

Personal experience

I was working in retail. I had joined a management training scheme and was considered a possible high flyer. At the age of 37, I certainly thought that if I didn't gallop through the initial management levels, then I would be past them by 40. Now, from the foothills of maturity, I can see that this was ridiculous.

On a training course, some shop managers took a question and answer session. One of the questions was: "What qualities do you need to be a good manager?" One of the managers answered: "Resilience. You need to be like a Weeble [a famous children's toy] – they always wobble but they don't fall down."

I couldn't work out what he was talking about. I found out two years later, the hard way. I had risen up the management ladder and was considered to be doing well. I was moved to a shop in a nearby town, but couldn't believe how different the working environment could be. It wasn't a happy time: I struggled and, in a dramatic fit of pique on one afternoon some six months later, I wrote my resignation. It was accepted.

Now I was in a mess: I needed a job and my status had fallen to zero. I had just thrown away the best company I would ever work for. I drove home, past my old shop. I parked and went back there: goodness knows what a sight I must have been. The manager was on the shopfloor. I begged him to take me back as a straightforward shop floor assistant. He was concerned that I would have trouble making the transition backwards – he need not have worried; I was in a state of shock.

A couple of weeks later, when the tears wouldn't stop coming, even on the shop floor, I was given some time off. It was a horrible time. I returned rested and ready to move up the ladder again, steadily and more slowly this time. It took a year, but I did it.

It gave me the biggest learning experience of my life. The actor and director Ben Affleck, who stood up at the Oscars to receive the Best Picture award in 2013 for *Argo* – 15 years after his first Oscar and through the highs and lows of film-making – said the following words:

"I want to thank them and I want to thank what they taught me, which is that you have to work harder than you think you possibly can. You can't hold grudges. It's hard but you can't hold grudges – and it doesn't matter how you get knocked down in life, because that's going to happen. All that matters is you gotta get up."

I understood completely.

Illustration

Suzanne had been married for 20 years. Her husband admitted to an affair, and she felt that her husband having an affair "wasn't fair". It wasn't, and she had every right to be upset and complain. Suzanne was a teacher and a new timetable revealed a change to a smaller classroom. That was unfair too.

One of her children was struggling, unlike his cousins. That was also unfair.

However, the language and manner that she used to describe her situation was not one of an adult – often she would talk like a sulky little girl.

Some gentle information-gathering revealed a root to her problem. Suzanne revealed feelings of unfairness in being the second daughter in the family, and having to put up with her older sister's 'hand-me-downs', including having the smaller bedroom. Those feelings had lasted decades. Now she felt like one of her husband's cast-offs, a secondhand teacher and a parent with a 'damaged goods' child. Emotionally, she needed to allow the competent and intelligent adult Suzanne to manage these varied situations, instead of her mini-me.

Reflection

Charles J. Sykes, author of *Dumbing Down Our Kids: Why American Children Feel Good about Themselves, but Can't Read, Write, or Add* wrote this set of rules for American high school students.

Rule 1: Life is not fair – get used to it!

Rule 2: The world won't care about your self-esteem. The world will expect you to accomplish something before you feel good about yourself.

Rule 3: You will *not* make $60,000 a year right out of high school. You won't be a vice-president with a car phone until you earn both.

Rule 4: If you think your teacher is tough, wait till you get a boss.

Rule 5: Flipping burgers is not beneath your dignity. Your grandparents had a different word for burger flipping – they called it opportunity.

Rule 6: If you mess up, it's not your parents' fault, so don't whine about your mistakes – learn from them.

Rule 7: Before you were born, your parents weren't as boring as they are now. They got that way from paying your bills, cleaning your clothes and listening to you talk about how cool you think you are. So before you save the rainforest from the parasites of your parent's generation, try delousing the closet in your own room.

Rule 8: Your school may have done away with winners and losers, but life *has not*. In some schools they have abolished failing grades and they'll give you as *many times* as you want to get the right answer. This doesn't bear the slightest resemblance to anything in real life.

Rule 9: Life is not divided into terms. You don't get summers off and very few employers are interested in helping you find yourself. Do that on your own time.

Rule 10: Television is *not* real life. In real life people actually have to leave the coffee shop and go to jobs.

Rule 11: Be nice to nerds. Chances are you'll end up working for one.

Chapter 5

'I can't do it': a wonderful sense of achievement

Happiness lies in the joy of achievement and the thrill of creative effort.

Franklin D. Roosevelt

A woman on the radio was asked if she drove a car. She said that she didn't: she had had one lesson and that, while her coordination was good, her steering was not, so she didn't have any more lessons. I would have loved to ask her some more questions:

- Why didn't she try again?
- What made her think that she wouldn't improve?
- Did she think she would be able to do it straight away?
- What was she frightened of?

It would be useful in life if adults could remember the following fact:

There is not one adult alive who hasn't consistently failed at something in the learning of a new skill. They never gave up, and were positively encouraged to try to succeed again. This could be where a very mini-me could be helpful pointing out these facts.

Dealing with failure

What is the connection between these three things?

1. A young man achieving success.

2. A group of middle-aged people not comfortable with technology.

3. Watching babies trying to walk.

The connection is learning to fail – learning to try again, learning that success only comes through failure.

1. The golfer Rory McIlroy's story is the stuff of legend. A young man who, under two years of age, loved his plastic golf clubs. Encouraged – and that word is crucial – by his parents, he played and practised for years. In one of his first major tournaments he was leading the pack. It was the 2011 US Masters Tournament and there was every indication that he would win on the last day – except that he didn't. The voice of doubt entered his consciousness and he lost the lead in a dramatic, if not humiliating, fashion. He failed in front of millions of people all over the world. Two months later he found himself in a similar position in the US Open Championship, leading the pack from day one and expected to win on the last day. This time the spectators and pundits had doubts. Did he fail again? No he didn't – it was a magnificent win.

To pick yourself up from a humiliating disaster and face the public again takes a high degree of emotional maturity. Rory still has moments of irrational behaviour, but his emotional brain is still maturing. As he said after the British Open in July 2013:

> But sometimes I feel I'm walking around out there unconscious. I just need to think more. I'm trying to focus and trying to concentrate. But I can't really fathom it at the minute, and it's hard to stand up

here and tell you guys what's really wrong. (*The Independent*, 19 July 2013)

2. I was with a group of middle-aged to older people, all belonging to a particular organisation. They were extremely competent professional people who are able to think independently and get things done. Some of these people don't have to use computers in their daily lives; they feel that social networking is too intrusive, and quietly grumble about the necessity for learning new stuff at their age. There is a divide beginning to show in certain organisations. There are those who are up to date with modern technology and want to carry on learning until the day they die; and there are those who are not. These days, whether people like it or not, using technology is vital for communication both inside and outside of organisations.

My favourite quote on embracing new technology comes from the Postmaster General in 1902: "The telephone is a wonderful invention. Every town should have one." It is not that the non-users cannot learn; it is that many are not inclined to try. They are frightened of failing and feeling 'stupid' – just like they did a long time ago. However, the language does not help: when I was first introduced to computers 20 years ago, all I heard about them was 'crashing' and stuff 'getting lost' – not helpful for confidence building.

3. On a visit to see my granddaughter and her big brother, it was a delight to see her walking – or rather falling over a great deal. Toddle, toddle, fall, get up again, toddle, toddle, fall, get up again, repeated hundreds of times in a day. We have nearly all done it. She was also learning to feed herself. The spoon went into her mouth with food... sometimes. It was wonderful observing a small child mastering skills. Now she is concentrating on drawing and using her scooter.

What can we conclude from these three analogies?

1. Rory McIlroy has practised for years and will go on practising. He will have successes and failures: he will learn from the failures and succeed again.

2. Some people in organisations will leave rather than learn.

3. My granddaughter will carry on failing, as she achieves small and large successes through life. Just like her grandmother.

Example

In the first workshop I gave in Australia, I asked for questions at the end. A man in his fifties put his hand up. "You've just made sense of my life," he said. With some surprise, I asked, "How?" He told the audience that when he was at primary school there was one teacher who used to stand behind him and say, "Collins, you are slow, but sure. Slow to learn and sure to fail." The man told the audience that every time he had looked for a job that he would like to apply for, he would just hear the teacher's words and not bother. He went on to say that he was going to change and not listen to that teacher anymore. I hope he did.

There are too many talented adults stuck in their lives because they allow their own inner voice of self-belief to be drowned out by an old voice belonging to someone else. A negative voice well past its sell-by date and belonging to someone who now may even be dead.

Personal experience

What can give us a huge, natural, punching-the-air 'high'? What about the sense of achievement that comes when we have tackled something difficult and succeeded? An easy task doesn't provide the same thrill at all. When I managed to pass an Open University exam at the age of 38, I ran around the room whooping and hollering in excitement. My family, all used to taking and passing exams by that time, thought my behaviour was over the top. They had absolutely no comprehension of the satisfaction it gave me – and why should they?

Learning and the brain

I love how quickly the brain can adapt. Staying in self-catering accommodation or driving a hire car: so much information to use in a quite different form to the way that your brain is used to. The brain adapts and before long, we are using the car or kitchen as if we have been used to it for years. The brain memory-matches. We may be looking at equipment we have never seen before, but we know what to do with it or can improvise. If we don't have a hammer, we will find something that is 'like' a hammer. If we don't have a cup to hold a drink, we will find something 'like' a cup.

Anyone who has hired a car knows the fundamentals well enough to drive it, but how many of us put the wipers on instead of the indicator? We may repeat that action a few times before our hands automatically make the correct choice. Repetitive action will 'hard wire' our brain and secure the neurological connections – that includes negative actions too. In a recent survey by the department store, John Lewis, 71% of parents admitted that they consult their children for technological advice, whether it is help online (for example, setting up social media profiles) or around the home. Children are keen to learn and not as afraid of making mistakes as adults. It is not that the adult cannot do it, they just don't want to 'fail' (although they do manage to learn when it is their mobile phone!).

Some words of warning

There is general acceptance now that praise and encouragement are helpful, and that filling a child with a sense of failure is unhelpful. The problem is that teaching is tipping the balance into giving a child unrealistic expectations. We praise a baby when it picks up a toy, but when do we stop? If we continue to praise a child for doing something that comes easily, the praise will be devalued. As adults, we need to move the boundaries of praise, along with the expectation of success. For example, a young child can be praised for a drawing: if that drawing doesn't get much better and the praise continues, the child will know that the praise is empty. Either that or they will not try to stretch themselves because they will be praised anyway. What I suggest is that the effort should be praised instead.

Example

Molly explained that at school she was a bright little girl, and that one day she was queuing at the teacher's desk to have her work marked. The teacher glanced at it and said, "Well, I don't have to look at this," and gave it a gold star. What did Molly take from that? Not a feeling of pride, but a feeling of 'I don't have to bother' which affected her through her schooldays. This was not what the teacher meant to happen at all.

Successful learning

Let's concentrate on the upside of learning: the sense of achievement that comes from being stretched, and beating our negative internal dialogue that tells us we cannot do it. It doesn't matter how large or small a success it is, just stop for a moment and remember when you had a 'Yes! I've done it!' moment. A time when you beat the odds. This is a memory you can use when you are next faced with a challenge.

In a workshop, Terri reported that she had stayed by the printer in the office, not giving in when the machine jammed, and had a great feeling of success when she managed to sort the problem out. If we want something different, we have to do something different.

Stations and airports make very good places to observe people under stress and their resulting behaviour.

I watched a middle-aged couple approach check-in at an airport. They were guided to the self-service machine. They looked at it, slightly bewildered. I could see that the woman was willing to work through the directions patiently, but not the man. He moved the woman aside and the stress levels became visible. He punched away randomly at various buttons. He then swore at the machine and finally kicked it. The woman looked around, she was embarrassed.

I believe that what the man was feeling is not dissimilar to those people who feel unable to get to grips with computers. They feel very uncomfortable with failing to grasp something the first time they have to do it. That feeling will be attached to a memory or memories that go back to original learning experiences. They become frightened of failing, of being yelled at, ridiculed and humiliated. So they don't try. It's such a shame, because not 'getting it' the first few times of doing something new is perfectly normal.

The developing child

During the early 1980s I supervised an unusual toddler group. It was only for two-year-olds, and without their parents. The children came for 90 minutes and they and their parents loved it. I had two helpers and around 20 toddlers. It is probably many people's idea of a nightmare, but it worked well. I was visited regularly by Social Services, who questioned my methods. It was the time of liberal thinking and allowing children to choose to do what they wanted in their own time. I was considered 'old school' as I set a routine and boundaries. The children thrived.

I was immersed in two-year-old behaviour, which is why I became intrigued two decades later, when I saw evidence of similar behaviour in adults with emotional health problems. I have a great affection for two-year-olds. Their minds are like blotting paper and they practise motor, language and social skills every day.

Then the child goes to school. There are lessons: some they like and are good at; some they don't like and find the concepts difficult to grasp. Natural talents begin to show, but not all are those that are fully understood in the classroom. Inside they may well start to feel angry and confused with receiving mixed messages. With some children, schoolday incidents can be traumatising – even ones that an adult would dismiss as being insignificant – and the effects can last for a lifetime. There is also a risk that a child who grows up believing that they are not any good can attract bullies, whether at work, socially or domestically.

The challenge of learning

David was illustrating a talk about learning when he told us that he used to sail a dinghy round a small, safe harbour on holiday. One day he ventured out of the harbour, hit very different waters and struggled to get back into port.

He told us that he learned more about sailing on that day than when he had just been pootling around in safe waters. A ship is safe in harbour, but this is not where a ship is meant to be.

Melanie, a woman in her thirties, sat in front of me, cross-legged on the chair. We talked through her options for changing her situation. It involved challenging her thoughts, and so changing her behaviours. She screwed up her face and said in a whine, "But it's hard!" At that moment I was not seeing a woman, but a child. "Yes, it is hard," I replied, "But we achieve nothing without challenging ourselves and then feeling a sense of achievement when we've succeeded – or given up, knowing that we've given it our best effort."

People can learn to change their reactions from childish ones from the past, to adult ones in the present. How many times should we keep trying until we give up? We have to accept a balance in how difficult a task should be, and that risks should be taken. There is no rule: common sense plays its part, as does an inner voice of honesty. Maturity in thinking plays its part too – it can inform us when to think about calling it a day. What should not play a part in our decision-making is someone else's negative voice from the past, informing our adult self with old, stale, out-of-date beliefs.

Personal experience

I was 50 years old and had promised to take my mother to visit her sister in America. This meant that I had to drive a hire car. I had never driven abroad, although I had been driving since I was 17 years old. I was not at all comfortable with the idea of driving, but the need for my ageing mother to see her older sister, possibly for the last time, was stronger than my wanting not to drive.

I made one concession: I said I would not hire a car from Los Angeles Airport, as I didn't think that would be a good idea. We caught a hotel bus instead, down the Californian coast, to our hotel.

The next day we went to the car rental agency and picked up a little red sporty number with automatic gears. My car at home was a 15-year-old Land Rover with basic manual controls. I had never driven an automatic car, or driven on the other side of the road, but I didn't have any option.

I am not going to pretend that the initial five-mile drive back to the hotel was easy – it wasn't. By the time we reached the hotel, my hands were so tightly gripped around the steering wheel that my knuckles had gone white. Then we drove the ten miles to my aunt. Scary, but better.

However, within days I was having the best driving experience ever, up and down the freeways, covering hundreds of miles like an old hand. There was even a tyre blowout and a change of car, but all managed without any problems. Well, almost: my cousin had warned me about stopping at road junctions. Stop means stop, not a rolling stop. A police motorcyclist stopped me, I wound down the window and received a strong lecture for doing 3mph. The look on his face when he eventually allowed me to speak was one to remember: he heard a full-blown English accent explain that I hadn't heard the siren because I had the pop group Queen turned up full volume on the radio. He tried hard not to smile and let me drive away, with a mild telling-off. The sense of satisfaction of driving in the USA was a real high: right up there with my Open University exam success and the police story has become a funny story to tell.

Illustration

Twenty-two-year-old Rob experienced plenty of negative feedback through his schooldays. He nearly gave up on several occasions. As an undergraduate he began to have dreams about his future; they seemed a little ambitious to some. He found a job that he wanted and applied for it. The support, encouragement and guidance from his friends and family was excellent.

However, the interview did not start well. Rob had put his full first name on the application form; as a result, that is how he was addressed. The problem was that only his mother called him by his full name, and he was thrown off track when addressed in the same way by the interviewer. He felt odd. He made a mess of the interview, and did not get the job.

Six weeks later Rob went for another interview in the same workplace, but for a different department. This time he had decided not to tell anyone, not to listen to advice, but just to be himself. He was offered the job and after 20 years and several promotions later, he is still there. In those six intervening weeks he had grown up. It was the man who went for that second interview, not the boy.

Reflection

When you want to achieve something yourself and encourage someone else, a little positive psychology can go a long way. A positive instruction will work better than a negative one, especially for a child – telling a child what to do, rather than what *not* to do – as will some positive visualisation. After a negative incident, telling yourself or a child "I knew it would be a disaster" is not going to be helpful. It means that the worst was imagined. For neurological reasons, the brain does not process negatives very well: the brain will read or hear the content rather than the command. So, the heavily advertised message 'Don't drink and drive' can be interpreted by the brain as 'Drink and drive.' Unfortunately, we seem to default so readily to giving commands negatively and wondering why they are ignored: "Don't do this, don't do that!" As a friend, Jenny, said:

"I was shouting at my children not to run by the side of the swimming pool. They were ignoring me, until I realised I wasn't telling them what to *do*, instead of what *not to do*. The instruction to 'walk slowly and safely' achieved instant results. It may seem obvious, but isn't."

Of course there will be times when the success you imagined and hoped for does not occur. Then comes the emotionally mature way of managing disappointment.

Try to picture the final result in your mind: the finished essay, the holiday, the passed exam. As you imagine it, the brain is already beginning to join the pathways together. Sports psychology is based on this aspect of neurobiology. This does not mean that you can leave doing the preparation and the revision, but you are making the final task a little easier.

One of my grandsons, Owen, told his father not to worry about buying a new golf bag for his holiday, as that was the prize in that day's competition and Owen was going to win it. He did. Owen had visualised success, which will have helped him considerably. If he had spent his time thinking, "I'll never win that", I doubt whether he would have done. My daughter has asked him to use the same approach to his exams.

Chapter 6

'You're not my friend anymore': social interaction, fun and friendship

If a man does not make new acquaintance as he advances through life, he will soon find himself left alone. A man, Sir, should keep his friendship in constant repair.

Samuel Johnson

How many times do we read about someone being 'a loner'? What does this imply? Sometimes the word is used in news reports to illustrate the lifestyle of someone who has been arrested for a horrific incident, often where personal harm to others is involved. What the report is suggesting is that the person does not mix with other people at work or socially. They do not have any friends.

No man is an island.

John Donne

Nor are we. We need other people to function in life. Even our basic needs of food, shelter, clothing, warmth and sanitation requite the input of an army of people. On a personal level we need to mix with people in order to function healthily. We need to mix with other people to learn peace, respect, compassion, honesty, sharing, trust, loyalty, fun and friendship. We start learning in the places of our first social gatherings, such as nurseries and with childminders. Our social circle then widens and, for most children, the neighbourhood, classroom and playground become the most common places to make friends.

We need friends. We need to feel wanted. We need to feel needed. Some people appear to have more friends than others; some people just have a couple of very close friends. Just one good friend who knows us well, can be enough, while others can be more of an acquaintance.

I sent my good friend Helen a birthday card. It said: "You'll always be my friend. You know too much!" Very true!

I feel that there is a difference between feeling lonely and feeling solitary. In the early 1990s, I chose to live on my own for the first time in my adult life. I have vivid memories of shutting the door of the flat behind me after a busy, fulfilling day at work, and feeling on my own. There was no one to make comments about a TV programme with, no one to discuss the evening news. No one with whom to share a glass of wine or meal. I felt solitary, certainly. But lonely? No – never. I was fortunate to have a network of friends fairly close by or down the end of the telephone. If it had been available, I am sure I would have been texting and using social networking, as I do now.

The situation I was in is familiar to those who find themselves living on their own for all sorts of reasons. Sometimes the shock of finding oneself on one's own has to be dealt with first before progress can be made. These days, food, wine, Facebook, Twitter or texting can all take the place of a friend. They are also all capable of being an addiction if our need for friendship is not fulfilled in more healthy ways. "He's a people pleaser", "She's a bit needy" or

"He's clingy" are negative descriptions about people who perhaps are trying too hard to be friendly. The more needy a person is, the more vulnerable they can be: it is possible to take advantage of them. The worst case scenario of this need being met unhealthily is grooming and subsequent abuse.

As I mentioned previously, the classroom and playground are frequently the first places where friendships are forged: if we are fortunate, some of those friendships will last a lifetime. However, these places are often where our strongest memories of falling out with friends can occur. Those memories and the messages that we received can be reminders of those times: "You're not my friend anymore" and "I hate you" are powerful statements that can last a long time if we allow them to.

At a school reunion 30 years after we had left, Nicki said, "As I've gone through life, I now realise that some of the nicest people I met were at school." I was fortunate to get to know one former pupil much better a few years after leaving school, when our workplaces turned out to be close to one another. Penny and I did not get on well together at school, but have become close friends since then and continue to support each other through the ups and downs of life.

Another group of girls were far too aloof and bohemian to be friends with: at the same reunion I realised that although their lifestyles had been very different from my own, I had allowed myself to be intimidated by them. Now I could see that they were just as ordinary as me, and that maybe they were trying just a bit too hard to be cool. Another extraordinary memory from that reunion was Jane, who had been precociously clever and in the top stream, telling me that the teachers had told her class not to mix with the girls in the bottom stream. "We thought you were stupid," she said, "but you're not, are you?"

Our memory-matches from those days can lead us to behave instinctively at any age. Names are probably the strongest matches from school; colours next.

The name of someone we loathed at school is unlikely to be the name that we give our child. The reverse is true too. My daughter is named after a friend at college, and my son after a good friend of his father's. I felt a twinge of pride when someone my son worked with called his son the same name. I knew he would not have done that if my son was an unpleasant person.

'Why do you dislike me?'

Example

I was in a meeting with 12 people, men and women. Our ages ranged over 35 years. A member of the organisation, Juliet, came into the room to inform us of something. She had spoken to the group briefly on a couple of other occasions, and no one had made any remarks afterwards. A perfectly ordinary woman in her thirties, with a regional accent, Juliet had an upbeat and friendly manner, and spoke to us in a normal voice. She left the room five minutes later.

One person expressed a dislike of the way Juliet had addressed the group: she felt that she had been patronised. Suddenly there were murmurings from around the room that became more vocal. The feelings about Juliet ranged from a strong dislike to thinking she was perfectly fine. Personally, I found her immensely irritating and had no idea that others held strong feelings – that is, until the bubble of politeness burst.

The matter passed and we went about our work, but I was fascinated with what I had just witnessed. The strong negative reaction to Juliet would be perfectly understandable if she had been unpleasant or threatening in any way, but she hadn't been at all.

Why do we take against people for what appears, sometimes, to be no particular reason? Of course, the opposite can be true as well. The clue lies in the emotion felt with something about them. There will be a memory-match and aspects of the person will be 'like' something in our past.

So what happened with Juliet? Each person would have had a different memory-match, and therefore a different emotion. Her tone of voice seemed to upset some people; I have a feeling that her physical appearance had been the trigger for others, perhaps her accent too. Thinking about my own reaction, I found her jollity too false, too ingratiating. It jarred. I feel that she was trying just a bit too hard – which is interesting in itself. Juliet held a prominent position, but I felt that possibly she was covering up an insecurity.

This type of situation is universal. People say, "I don't know why so and so doesn't like me." The person doing the disliking may not even really know why.

The reason for disliking someone can appear irrational, but with a little thought, generally the reason can become obvious. It can be less so for behaviours called 'instinctive' or 'having a sixth-sense'.

A head of department, Liz, came to see me when I was working for a large local authority. She enjoyed her job, but found one particular member of the team difficult to get on with: this person was good at their work and reliable, but there was something annoying about her.

I explained how our brain can memory-match, and that certain memory-matches can give us a strong emotion. She came back the next day and told me:

> I've got it. Sitting on the train going home, I was thinking about what you said. Snap! Her tone of voice is exactly like my mother's. I feel about five years old in her presence.

If the memory-match has an element of fear attached, then the brain's alarm system may sound a warning. A serious warning can lead to a panic attack: that is when we need to take a moment to consider whether the threat is real, imagined, or just remembered.

An interesting workshop exercise to illustrate the emotions attached to memory-matches can be to use certain objects or words and ask for immediate reactions. At one workshop I remember saying the name 'Dave'. The reactions ranged from nothing in particular to loathing about a brother-in-law, to tears of grief over a dog that had recently died. The smell from a bunch of lavender evoked a sad memory from one person of visiting someone dying in hospital, and a happy memory from another of a cat rolling in a shrub outside a grandmother's house.

Personal experience

I was sitting with a man I was fond of. I gazed at him. He looked up and spoke sharply to me, telling me to stop looking at him like that. This happened well before I had ever learned about how the brain functioned, but I recognised that I was on the receiving end of something that didn't belong to me. It had happened before in my life – so I challenged him.

It turned out that my loving look was 'like' a way that a previous girlfriend had looked at him. She turned out to be a little emotionally unstable, and my father had mental health problems. Snap! A match had happened in his brain – a pity that it was the wrong one. Fortunately, talking about it solved any problems that might have arisen. However, using that example, it is easy to understand how decision-making can become skewed on occasion, and unreliable opinions formed.

Advertisers, marketers and designers use memory-matching all the time. Without customers being able to match memories to the senses, there would be no marketing or advertising industries. We may match girlfriends with mothers or sisters, and boyfriends with fathers or brothers – with differing results. How many people do we know who find a new partner that looks very similar to their ex?

Mistaken matches

Someone I know called Rita used to get irritated in the 1960s and 1970s when scriptwriters used her name for a stereotypical peroxide-blonde 'common' woman. Now they use Sharon, Tracy or Kylie, which must annoy women with those names too. For Rita, having the same name as a traffic warden in a song by The Beatles didn't help either; but when people do get her name wrong, they call her Ruth. They hear the first letter, see her or hear her voice, and always match it to Ruth.

I once introduced myself to a complete stranger, a man in his sixties, who took my hand and then burst into tears. "That was the name of my neighbour when I was a little boy. She was the only person who was kind to me." A poignant case of emotional immaturity.

As the saying goes, 'Don't judge a book by its cover' – but we do, don't we? We are all guilty of making judgements about people that may not be based on anything other than what, exactly?

For example, murder creates strong emotional reactions. In a famous case, the murder of Joanna Yeates in Bristol in 2010, there was a news report in two tabloid newspapers about Christopher Jeffries, Yeates's landlord, who lived in the same building. Because he looked eccentric, people thought him guilty of the crime, but he wasn't. He sued the newspapers successfully. In another case in 2000, a local community became emotionally aroused and attacked the house belonging to a paediatrician, Yvette Cloette. Unfortunately, the ringleaders had only heard the syllable 'paed', and mistakenly thought that the occupant was a paedophile.

Our need for support

Support groups can be a great source of friendship in times of need. Someone experiencing a traumatic life event can feel very alone, and a support group for that particular life event can be found, either locally or online, or both. These groups can bring great comfort and I support their work. To know that you are not the only person to feel as you do can help the healing process. However, I sound a warning: there is a downside to support groups. What if the person's life event becomes their *raison d'être*? It can be difficult to move on.

For example, two carers of partners with Alzheimer's disease had been recently widowed. Katie and Martin found the local Alzheimer's group an enormous support. Martin has chosen to stay with the group to help with fundraising, while Katie has been recommended to 'move on'. This is difficult, when members of the group have become friends and belonging to the group has given life a meaning and purpose.

One of my tutors, Richard and his wife, Tessa, had experienced a shocking, sudden infant death, and found great support in a local group. However, after a while, Richard realised that he and Tessa needed to leave the group, as the sole topics of conversation were the dead children of the group members. He knew that they needed to move forward in their lives.

Alice found great support in a local group for people experiencing depression. After a few months, she felt much better and was able to engage with outside life again. She liked the group members, but found that the dynamic had changed during the time she had attended. The group was picking away at old wounds in a toxic atmosphere, whereas she was healing and ready to move away. They were genuinely pleased with her progress, but suddenly she wasn't one of them anymore. Strong emotions can keep people where they are, including the fear of leaving a comfort zone.

Influences from the past

My clients have often expressed that one of their parents or grandparents didn't like them and the relationship was difficult, sometimes abusive. I would ask them if their parents got on well: generally the answer was negative. I then asked them, "Which person do you most resemble?" The answer would be the kinder person. I suggested that the difficult parent may be 'dumping' their own relationship frustrations on the child.

I grew up with the ringing tones of "You're just like your father" in a none too complimentary manner. Of course, with hindsight, I know what that was all about. My father caused huge problems in the family, and if any of my behaviours resembled (memory-matched) my father's in any way, the outburst was triggered.

Freud calls this matching type of behaviour 'transference'. If the consequences are negative, I call it 'emotional dumping' – which reminds me of a story.

Two monks approached a riverbank and saw a woman needing to cross. One monk put the woman on his shoulders and waded across to the other bank, where he put her down. They proceeded on their way. At nightfall, when they were permitted to speak, the other monk asked: "How could you touch and even pick up that woman when you know it's against our order? How could you do that?" "Easy," said the monk. "When I reached the other side. I put her down. You're still carrying her."

So many people, so many lives, so many memory-matches, so much emotional baggage.

The need for friendship is a powerful need, and the way that people can be manipulated and abused in the name of friendship is common. If our self-respect is not very high, then we can become vulnerable. As mentioned previously, the worst scenario is that of young girls and women being groomed: how powerful it can be to have someone show interest in you, express a liking or even love of you. They approve of you. They give you gifts. Life at home or school isn't much fun, and you feel lonely. Someone shows you approval. You are trapped in their lair.

This is not only for sex. I have known manipulative friendships happen in educational establishments and workplaces: one person is only in the friendship to manipulate the other, and emotional blackmail can take hold. The threat of withdrawal of the friendship can be a powerful motivator for making some unhealthy decisions. There is also a connection with bullying here. In my experience, bullies of all ages are like frightened small children inside. They have worked out how to wield some sort of power over others and use it. If asked, I would always have said that I had never been a bully. Only with hindsight can I now admit that perhaps two people could have said they were bullied by me. With hindsight I can say that I was 11 and 15 at the time and honestly didn't really understand what I was doing. I wish I could go back and apologise. Bullying is about feeling some sort of superiority... The question then is, why would one want to feel superior?

Illustration

Remember Neil and his half-empty buckets? He spoke about how he hated the way he behaved when his wife was going out without him. It could be when she was going out to have some fun with a friend, or with the children for a half-term outing. He would go and sit in a particular chair, pout and sulk. He recognised what he was doing, and knew that it irritated his wife – but felt that he couldn't stop it. Ultimately he said that he felt lonely and left out.

As Neil's body language was that of a child when he talked about these events, it seemed a simple question to ask him to engage with the little boy that he felt like at these times, and tell me what was going on in his life then.

The emotional brain can memory-match quickly. His brain did. Snap! His mother was a piano teacher and had taught him to play. As an adult, he played well; however, the memory-match had been of his mother saying that he wasn't allowed to go out to play with his friends – he had to stay in and practise the piano.

So the little boy, who felt left out of the fun and games that his friends were having, grew up and became a well-qualified member of the legal profession. His IQ was not in question. His EQ? At certain times he felt like a lonely little boy of nine.

The solution? Neil recognised that he could 'grow up' and behave like an adult. If he couldn't go with them, then he could let them go with his good wishes, and maybe some spending money – and that is what he did.

Reflection

People come into your life for a reason, a season or a lifetime. When you figure out which one it is, you will know what to do for each person.

When someone is in your life for a reason, it is usually to meet a need you have expressed. They have come to assist you through a difficulty; to provide you with guidance and support; to aid you physically, emotionally or spiritually. They may seem like a godsend, and they are. They are there for the reason you need them to be.

Then, without any wrongdoing on your part or at an inconvenient time, this person will say or do something to bring the relationship to an end. Sometimes they die. Sometimes they walk away. Sometimes they act up and force you to take a stand. What we must realise is that our need has been met, our desire fulfilled; their work is done. The prayer you sent up has been answered and now it is time to move on.

Some people come into your life for a season, because your turn has come to share, grow or learn. They bring you an experience of peace or make you laugh. They may teach you something you have never done. They usually give you an unbelievable amount of joy. Believe it. It is real. But only for a season.

Lifetime relationships teach you lifetime lessons; things you must build upon in order to have a solid emotional foundation. Your job is to accept the lesson, love the person, and put what you have learned to use in all other relationships and areas of your life. It is said that love is blind, but friendship is clairvoyant.

Brian Andrew (Drew) Chalker

Chapter 7

'Go away – I hate you': the need for love

I was born with an enormous need for affection and a terrible need to give it.

Audrey Hepburn

There is a book called *Never Kiss in a Canoe: Words of Wisdom from the Golden Age of Agony Aunts* by Tanith Carey. It is a collection of answers given by agony aunts over the last 100 years. From the distance of years, the letters make for mostly amusing reading, but they are tinged with sadness. The advice was what was thought best at the time and by people who hoped they were helping others – and this is no different today. In decades to come, will people laugh at today's problem pages? Here is an example.

Q: Do you believe that petting a child is bad for it?

A: Yes, decidedly I do. A child gets very much attached to Mother (or Nurse) who feeds and baths it. It should be the mother's aim to prevent the child getting too attached to her and fondling the child too often has the opposite effect.

The child who gets all the fondling is always looking for it in everybody and it is miserable without it.

The adult who is always recounting his ills and looking

for sympathy is the outcome of too much cuddling in childhood. That is why psychologists say too much mother love is harmful.   *Modern Woman*, 1929

We can find it amusing to read, but there is a serious side to this advice. With more than 40 years of experience, children who are "looking for fondling in others" are doing so because their fundamental need for affection and touch has *not* been met within the close family – quite the opposite to being met too much.

We can laugh (or cry) at how outdated this advice is. Or is it? A few years ago, I attended a family conference with social workers and foster parents. The discussion was of how inappropriate an eight-year-old boy's behaviour was with the temporary foster mother. The foster mother, who was of a slim build, reported that the boy wanted to sit on her lap and snuggle into her chest. I was horrified as the discussion continued. I suggested that as the birth mother had a capacious bosom and the boy enjoyed cuddles with his mum, that he was, in fact, in his confused state, looking for some comfort from his foster mum – not that his behaviour meant that he should be put on a sex register. The conversation stopped. The 'professionals' looked at me. It was obvious that no one had even considered this as a possibility. There was a shuffling of papers and the discussion moved on. Is there is something crucially missing from their training?

However, there is another side to this argument. Those children who may have had their needs met, but in a more unhealthy way, can have difficulty adjusting emotionally as adults. It does not take too much of a leap of imagination to see what may happen if these unmet childhood needs are carried into adulthood. If the emotional need of giving and receiving of love is missing or abused in childhood, is it possible for an adult with immature emotional growth to be looking for it when they are older?

I am not making excuses for the behaviour of paedophiles of either sex. This is where personal responsibility should be taken into account. But I am suggesting reasons for that behaviour. Of course, as in most behaviours, there is then the interesting matter as to why some people who have experienced trauma appear 'damaged' for life and some do not. I believe that most paedophiles could identify a time in their lives when they were abused or neglected. On the other hand, not all abused children grow up to be paedophiles. The difference? I suggest emotional maturity.

In 2006, the then Deputy Prime Minister, John Prescott, a man in his late sixties, was discovered to have had an affair with his much younger secretary, Tracey Temple. She had written a diary that was made public, earning her a great deal of money but also a great deal of ridicule, and one wonders whether she now thinks the financial gain was worth it. The actress Maxine Peake researched the diaries as background for her role in a film about the affair:

> What struck the actress most forcibly was the breathless, girly tone of the writing. "She's a woman in her early forties, but they read like teenage diaries. She's slightly naive and immature. But … she was an army baby and her father left her when she was young. She was looking for attention and affection – which gives you a sense of why she'd fall for a big lump like Prescott." (*The Independent*, 27 February 2007)

The importance of touch

Touch is one of the five major senses. It is important: a loving touch or a hug can bring so much comfort. In a time of great distress, I was in a church. Slowly and silently, tears began to roll down my face. The woman next to me, who I barely knew, just reached over and held my hand. She said nothing. It meant the world to me. I wasn't alone, and she understood: so simple and so effective.

Touch does not have to be human. Animals can provide a healthy outlet for touch, and stroking can be so therapeutic. It is no coincidence that taking pets into care homes can provide positive results: the very act of stroking will calm one's breathing down. There are many people who have lost faith in their fellow man, who find that the unconditional love that a pet can give fills the gap. This is also why the death of a pet can cause a person more grief than the death of a human being. Moreover, children who have communication and behavioural problems can often respond to a pet more effectively than an adult. (Knowing that we would need companionship, my husband once joked that if ever we find ourselves on our own, we would acquire a dog instead of looking for some human love and affection.)

In the lexicon of social work, we have 'appropriate touching'. This has been taken to a questionable level, and there are now rigid rules as to what a teacher or leader can do with a small child. As someone who ran a toddler group, the thought of not being able to instinctively comfort a young child in an open area fills me with horror. The balance has gone too much the other way.

The need to give and receive love can be met in inanimate objects too. If we are not receiving the love that we should, then we look to get our needs met elsewhere. Often, a child can find those feelings with a cuddly toy or a blanket. We are touching something soft, maybe warm and with a familiar smell. I wonder if this is where an adult need for soft toys comes from?

The York Press newspaper reported the case of a young man aged 20: he had been imprisoned for 16 months because he has a shoe fetish and grabbed a high-heeled shoe from a woman while she was wearing it. He had done this before.

While I acknowledge that the incidents could be frightening for the woman, there is something slightly amusing in the weirdness of this fetish.

However, I despaired. Sixteen months in jail: exactly how is that going to stop this young man's behaviour? He is a poorly educated man of 20, with a younger emotional age. It's a fetish, an addiction. In one of the reports I read, the authorities spoke of not being able to find out exactly why it was happening.

I thought of another case a few years ago in 2007 that was not dissimilar. A man with a fetish and uncontrollable behaviour was frightening people in his search for satisfaction. I wrote a letter to *The York Press* and it was made the lead letter:

Sir,

The Press writes about Norman Hutchins, "once again", as he is jailed for three years. (Sept 4th 2007)

I am not excusing Mr Hutchins' behaviour, but maybe there is a reason, which it doesn't take a genius to work out. The judge is wrong, it can be changed.

Mr Hutchins is on a desperate search for something. He keeps looking but doesn't find it. In his case it would appear to be some sort of comfort, security and attention. I would guess that at some point in his upbringing, these vital childhood needs were met with something connected with health, doctors, hospitals or similar. As an adult he, like all of us, still needs comfort, security and attention. But as an adult, he hasn't been able to get these needs met in a healthy way, only and ironically, in an unhealthy way. Emotionally he's a frightened child.

There are many prisoners who are only back in prison because they have many of their needs met in prison and not in the outside world, e.g.: friendship, community, boundaries and security.

If we look at the Strensall gangs, it's all about getting needs met, but in an anti-social way. Attention, fun, security, friendship, status, sense of community, sense of achievement, feeling valued, meaning and purpose. Until these children's needs are met in a healthy way, the gangs will thrive and some of them too will end up in prison.

I expect there will be many readers who may dismiss my words, but I wonder how many readers are this very day seeking feelings of comfort, security and attention in their behaviours. They will be drinking and eating unhealthily, because they are searching for a feeling of comfort. They are spending money on gambling and on goods that they can't afford, but it's giving them a meaning and purpose. They will seeking sex-filled thrills to feel loved and valued. They will be working to a point of exhaustion, not because of needing the money, but because they are searching for a feeling of being good enough. Maybe they do need the money to pay for goods that really they only want, but don't actually need, but these goods provide them with a feeling of status amongst their peers. Are we so different from Mr Hutchins?

A fetish sounds seedy, but grabs headlines. Mr Hutchins has an addiction, because he is craving a feeling he once had and is trying to find again. He won't ever find it though, because it belongs in the past. He is not alone as he chases rainbows. There is no pot of gold.

Yours sincerely, etc.

Replaying the past

Personal experience

I'm 5ft 8ins tall. I'm also outgoing and tactile. This means that without being fully aware, I can be a little overpowering for some people. I attempt to be self-aware, but can sometimes forget and invade personal space.

I also like cuddles. "Why do you hug so tightly?", a boyfriend once asked. I had no idea. I have some idea now: in my teenage years I had an absent father, but in my younger childhood he was present. A tall figure, he used to sit and watch the cricket on TV, leaning forward with his elbows on his knees. This made a little shelter for me to sit in. When I have memory-matched to a feeling, that is the memory I have: one of being protected, although the reality was that as a father and husband he was somewhat lacking in certain major areas of responsibility. Maybe that is where I got a liking for cricket, too.

There weren't many men in my home and school environment, but when I did start to go out in mixed company, it was the taller boys I liked. The problem was that, generally, the one I was with wasn't enough, and I used to flirt in an outrageous way: so immature, so needy. Nowadays, I expect I would take matters further and be sexually promiscuous, but I wasn't, and I am grateful for a degree of self-discipline that came from somewhere. However, I am pretty sure that my unconscious search for a man who could protect me arose from the childhood experience.

But I am not the only one. Men and women have a personal radar, looking for figures either to match the loved parent, or to replace the one that they never had or lost – and their expectations are thwarted. How can someone else be all that we need them to be? This is one of the myriad reasons behind failed marriages.

Illustration

My husband Alex and I were walking along a road near our home. It was a winter's evening, cold and dark. A young lad, around 16 years old, was on a bicycle, weaving in and out of the oncoming traffic in a most alarming way. He appeared to have a death wish: if he continued, someone was going to get hurt, whether it was himself or a car driver. We managed to draw him to one side and talk quietly with him. We didn't feel that a reprimand would do any good, as he appeared distressed in some way. We listened to him, and he calmed down.

Someone had called the police, and soon a van drew up. They recognised him and bundled him into the van, kicking and screaming – so much for us calming him down. I later learned from a social worker friend that he was well known in the town as a troublesome lad. I will never forget the words he kept repeating, as we were listening to him: "I just want my mum to love me."

Annie had a drink problem. She asked my advice. She told me that once she had dealt with her present problems, she would address the fact that she knew that she drank too much and was probably an alcoholic. She was thinking of attending a local alcohol centre. I suggested that while support groups could certainly help, identifying what she was looking for through alcohol might be a good starting point. I asked her what she was looking for at the bottom of the glass. She immediately said: "My mother's love."

Ken was in his fifties and a chief executive of a multi-million pound organisation. He had an alcohol problem, and his wife and daughter had had enough of his behaviour. As soon as he had a drink, they ignored him. He wanted to be with them, but they didn't want to be with him. As he related this, he appeared to shrink in the chair. Ken also told me about his mother and the demands she still made on his life. We talked about how he felt when he was drinking: "I just want to be loved by my mother." Ken was a big man, in all senses of the word at work, but a sad, misunderstood little boy at home.

Marianne married for a second time. It was her husband Rick's second marriage too. She assured me that everything was great between them, and that they enjoyed a full, healthy relationship. The wedding day was fun, but that night he didn't want to make love – he didn't ever again. What transpired over a very difficult couple of years before they separated was that all he wanted was mothering, and as Julie said after their separation, "I didn't marry my lover to turn into his mother." The world being a small place, and in a completely different public place, I met Rick's sister. Shelley was another troubled soul who was trying every therapy under the sun to find some unmet need. This included rebirthing.

> *I've always told young women who think they are looking for Mr Right that they are looking for Mr Wrong, because that is who the exciting, charismatic charmer turns out to be. It is profoundly destructive behaviour. If you get raped by a complete stranger in your bedroom it's truly shocking. But if you are raped by someone you think you are being intimate with, which is what it is, then you have been done in, you are badly hurt and it will affect your self-esteem. Women are so needy for love that they will interpret the most cynical behaviour as affection.*
>
> **Germaine Greer**

Reflection

Soroptimist International of Great Britain and Ireland supports women and girls. The Yorkshire region created a bookmark with the lists shown below on either side. The Co-operative Society sponsored the initiative, and thousands have already been given out to young women (see Appendix 2).

The lists were created as part of an anti-grooming initiative, but most of the behaviours listed could be used in all sorts of relationships: parent–child, employer–employee or teacher–student. I would add that the person whose behaviour follows 'Loves me' displays emotional maturity, and the list for 'Loves me not' shows emotional immaturity.

Loves me	Loves me not
Makes me feel safe	Is jealous
Makes me feel comfortable	Is possessive
Listens to me	Tries to control me
Values my opinions	Gets violent, loses temper quickly
Supports what I want to do in life	Always blames me
Is truthful with me	Is sexually demanding
Admits to being wrong	Keeps me from seeing friends and family
Respects me	Makes all the decisions
Likes that I have other friends	Embarrasses me in front of others
Makes me laugh	Hits me

Trusts me	Makes me cry
Treats me as an equal	Is always 'checking up' on me
Respects my family	Takes my money and other things
Understands my need for time alone or with family	Threatens to leave me if I don't do what I'm told
Accepts me as I am	Teases, bullies and puts me down

Chapter 8

'Let me do it!': control

You have power over your mind – not outside events. Realise this, and you will find strength.

Emperor Marcus Aurelius

Susan and Jack were getting married. It was a second marriage for them both. While it would have been easy to blame their previous partners for all the mistakes made in their previous relationships, they were mature enough to know that they were not without some blame themselves. They discussed elements of their characters that may not have helped the relationships. This took honesty and putting blame to one side. It also took emotional maturity. Jack said that he felt that always wanting to feel in control may have caused some problems. A little more discussion uncovered the fact that Jack was stopped from doing things that he wanted to do by his parents. As a result, in adulthood when he was told that he couldn't do something or somebody else tried to organise him, sometimes his emotional mini-me would take over and he could become awkward, before thinking the matter through. Susan also disliked being told what to do, but for different reasons arising from her childhood, and had fought hard to get her own way, causing problems in her previous relationship. When I last met them they assured me that they were still happily married.

Whatever it may look like to an outsider, when we lose control we can feel pretty awful. Out-of-control thoughts can lead to out-of-control behaviours. Then we lose self-esteem, self-confidence and certainly self-discipline and self-respect. No wonder it feels better to blame anyone or anything but ourselves for our actions. Stopping and taking control of our emotions in a situation can be hard work. Generally, though, we will gain that self-control, self-esteem, self-confidence and self-respect – plus we have no problem taking responsibility for our actions.

Fear and the human brain

The human brain has an in-built alarm system for survival purposes: the amygdala. It is almond-shaped and sits in the emotional brain, in the right brain hemisphere (see Appendix 1). The amygdala has been present in the human brain since the evolution of man: it is responsible for our 'fight, flight or freeze' reaction. If our ancestors had not been able to deal with trouble by fighting, running away quickly or staying stock still, we would not be here today. It represents pure survival instincts.

Remember the old smoke alarms in homes? They were fairly primitive and could not tell the difference between a puff of cigarette smoke and a chip pan fire. They are now programmed to be a little more sophisticated – certainly, they are more efficient, but like human beings, still not perfect. Our personal alarm is still primitive, not sophisticated and sometimes cannot tell the difference between real or perceived danger. It can be set off with just a puff of encouragement, generally the slightest hint of fear. This kind of reaction can be responsible for the spectrum of traumatic reactions in animals, human and otherwise – from mild feelings of anxiety to panic attacks, phobias and full-blown post-traumatic stress disorder (PTSD; see Chapter 11). Perhaps this is okay if we are under attack verbally or physically, but ninety-nine percent of the time can lead to an overreaction, and possibly troublesome consequences for ourselves. Sometimes we can make unhelpful judgements or decisions. We can panic or embarrass ourselves.

For example, I was taking a plane trip in America. The crew giving the safety announcement said: "Please help children put on the life vest first – or those behaving like children." A great illustration of how emotional arousal triggered by fear can cause immature behaviour. It is important to the understanding of how, in given situations, we can lose control so easily; whereas it tends to take a little more effort to take control.

At this point, we should recall how children react: pretty much spontaneously, until either they are spoken to by an adult, or grow up and learn to understand to control themselves. There is a big clue here to immature behaviours. So what happens if the adult brain is still being controlled by the child's emotional reactions? It is easy to work out, and usually it is not anything helpful. Children need guidance until they can take responsibility for themselves. At what age does that happen? Well, brain development is individual. And as this book has shown, some adults of mature years still find it difficult.

Illustration

Is there anything more impulsive than the way that small children will run out into the road, totally unaware of danger? I watched a road safety lesson with a primary school class of eight-year-olds. The children were being taught how to cross the road safely on their own; everyone wore bright yellow high-visibility jackets. After being taught, 'Stop, Look and Listen' and being walked through the lesson with an adult, they did it on their own and crossed to the other side of the road. When they had completed the crossing safely, another adult praised them or corrected them on anything that they might have forgotten to do. If necessary, they had to repeat the action until it was successfully completed.

I have not observed adults going around in their day-to-day lives, crossing roads still dressed in yellow jackets; neither are they attached to another adult holding them on reins, as toddlers can be. As adults we self-regulate. So if we are doing it on the public highway, why can't we do it in other walks of life?

What happens if the adult brain is still being controlled by the child's emotional reactions in certain situations? Imagine a role reversal in the road safety class, and visualise an under-five who doesn't know about 'Stop, Look and Listen' taking control of an adult crossing the road – we wouldn't allow it. So why do we listen to our mini-me in other circumstances? Why haven't we learned to ignore our 'mini-me' for our own safety?

So, how can we begin to learn to take control instead of losing control, and how does the road safety lesson help?

Step 1: STOP – recognise a feeling or emotion that is beginning to rise.

Step 2 : LOOK – what are the consequences of the action you are about to take? (Warning: It is very easy at this stage to be hijacked by a childish voice saying things like "I want it, and I want it now!" or "No, I won't!")

Step 3: LISTEN – Say "Freeze!" to yourself, then choose an instant calming technique, from breathing or distraction (see Appendix 3).

Example

Nine-year-old Harry was commended at school for showing mature behaviour under provocation. An argument about football arose in the playground and Harry could feel himself becoming angry. Realising that the outcome of losing his temper may not be helpful, Harry walked away, despite the situation 'not being fair'. A teacher observed the incident and Harry was commended. He showed unusually emotionally mature behaviour for a nine-year-old. How can we take, and not lose, control? What did that little boy do?

The radio and TV presenter, Richard Bacon, said that he swore in daily life but self-edited on the radio. I liked that expression, 'self-edited'. It is another form of self-control and being self-disciplined. I also self-edit, especially in front of children, although I remember well when I didn't: it was a work situation, when I swore to fit in – silly now in hindsight, and immature, but understandable.

Speed of thought

Sitting on the London Underground, I was taken with an advertisement that ran over several sites along the carriage wall above the windows. There was a squiggle and the tagline read: "A Train of Thoughts". I have long forgotten what it was advertising, but I have not forgotten the idea, and used it many times. After all, "Are we on the right track?" is a well-used expression.

I once lived near a busy railway station, with fast, non-stop trains passing through and slower trains stopping at all the stations. The brain has different sizes of tracks for thoughts. Some are fast and non-stop, and some are slower, where you can take in the wider picture and have time for reflection. The fast, non-stop train of thought gathers speed and reaches its destination more quickly. Imagine going into a tunnel where you cannot get perspective, and cannot get off the train. This is fine if the destination is actually one that we want to get to, but we feel 'stupid' if it isn't.

With the slower, more thought-provoking train of thoughts, we have more choice and ability to get off if they are going in the wrong direction. However, most of the time we have a choice. Even if we have got onto the fast train, we can pull our 'internal emergency cord' and stop the train. Anybody can do this to stop themselves from doing something that they may come to regret (although we should note that the ability to do so diminishes under the influence of any type of mind-altering substance).

A useful brain fact to remember is that most of the time we cannot control the first thought that comes into our head because it is random – but we can take control over the second and subsequent ones.

Control techniques

Mind–body connections provide their own resources or tools to deal with times when emotional arousal may be unhelpful in a given situation. The tools are more effective if they are used early: for example, before the arousal level becomes too high. High arousal requires more effort to achieve a result, but it will still work. The secret is to practise these techniques when you are not feeling stressed or out of control, then they will come more easily when you need to use them.

Exercise

Step 1: Recognise a feeling when the resulting thoughts or actions may not be helpful, if allowed to develop.

Step 2: Say "Freeze!" to yourself, then choose a brain game from the instant calming techniques of breathing, distraction or exercise – whatever is suitable for the environment in which you find yourself (see Appendix 3).

Step 3: Practise, practise, practise!

To give an example: a colleague, Joy, adapted the natural brain reaction of switching brain hemispheres to a brain game for children in school who were becoming unruly and excluded from the classroom. The children responded well and the teachers approved. When Joy mentioned this technique in a peer group meeting, it was eagerly adopted by her colleagues. It is such a simple but effective tool for use by everybody, whatever their ages, and has been adapted for use as a distraction technique.

Illustration

Joy helped Leo recognise the initial feelings of emotional arousal in his body and scale them from one to ten. Leo was then taught to recognise when the feelings were lower on the scale, and take action before they reached higher on the scale and he lost control. In class, when Leo started to experience feelings at the lower end of the scale, he held up a card and the teacher allowed Leo to go out of the classroom. Leo stood outside the classroom doing a brain game exercise of his choice. He became aware of the reduction of his emotional arousal, and when Leo felt back in control, he would go back into class. He felt a real sense of achievement and the teacher was pleased too. A positive result for all involved.

We can change our reactions, and quickly too. We can change unhelpful behaviours, but sometimes we can believe "that's how we are" and that change is not possible. Sam was a young man who believed that he had done some permanent damage to his brain by drug use. I could not say whether he had done so or not, but I could tell him that neurologists talk of the plasticity of the brain: that it can be remoulded and adapt in new ways.

He didn't believe me. Fortunately the house dog came to my assistance. It had been in a road accident as a puppy and lost one leg. It was quite something to see a large poodle moving around on three legs, but he did it well. I turned to the dog and asked Sam whether the dog's brain had adapted to a different way of working. He had to agree that it had done, and done it well. He then believed me.

Possibly due to the brain's plasticity, the inventor of the Nintendo brain-training games, Dr Ryuta Kawashima, appears to have had some success in working with people with dementia to stimulate memory. Much of the millions of dollars he has made have been put into a research centre an Institute of Aging and Cancer at Tohoku University in Japan, which is attached to the Institute of Development, Aging and Cancer. But Japan's Ministry of Health is refusing to fund large-scale trials. Dr Kawashima says, "Many doctors are not happy with our results because if they use our method, they can't sell drugs. This is a very big market in Japan and they would be losing a lot of money."

Force of habit

What is a habit? A behaviour that was not in place before, but has now been practised so many times that it is habitual. I used to point out that, while it is difficult for people with diabetes to change their diets, they manage, otherwise they could die. However, I come across many people with life-limiting problems who find it difficult to take control of the situation, take responsibility for changing themselves, and go into denial. Ann Moir of Brainsexmatters.com contentiously suggests that denial behaviour can be more male-brained. Is it? Doctors have told me that generally men are slower at going to their GPs with chronic symptoms. In articles on health pages men often admit that "my wife nagged me" or "I tried to ignore it". Is that a brain function or just 'stiff upper lip'? Nature or nurture? When ill-health does occur, some people will blame anything and everybody but themselves, although feeling bad, because they know it is really their responsibility. When minor problems become major ones, it leads to further distress all round, and costs the health service millions of pounds a year.

We can become addicted to thinking and doing things in the same way, because changing and taking control means effort. Addictions are also called habits, as in "They've got a habit". The only habit we have is doing something over and over again until it is automatic behaviour: this is great if the outcome is helpful, but not if otherwise.

Personal experience

Habits can also become rituals. When my husband, Alex, asked me why I was adamant, at our first Christmas together, that I wanted something done a certain way, I told him it was because it had always been done like that. He responded with: "That's a very good reason for changing, then".

Maturity and self-discipline

There is much talk in the news on the need for parenting for out-of-control children. I read as much on the subject as I can. I often think that so much of it could have been written in any section of a newspaper dealing with the present problems in society. If the words 'we' or 'ourselves' are used instead of 'child' or 'children', then the content could address the problems being experienced in schools, with binge drinking and other addictive behaviours, spiralling debt, a range of anger problems and family breakdown, to name but a few subjects that make the radio, television, newspapers and magazines on a regular basis.

What goes around comes around, and it is interesting to read ideas promoted in the early twenty-first century that were part of my training as a nursery nurse in the late 1960s. I also see the same ideas promoted in the *Supernanny* or 'taming toddler' TV programmes: that is, of setting boundaries of what is acceptable and unacceptable behaviour. (In these programmes it is always the parent that has to change their behaviour in order for the child to change – it could not be otherwise.)

It is childcare training and subsequent work with the under-fives, especially with the under-threes, that has helped inform my thinking on this subject. I have observed out-of-control adults who, in certain situations, appear unable to use self-discipline.

We have CCTV cameras in town centres that now 'talk' to anyone displaying anti-social behaviour, and a major supermarket chain is going to give out nutritional advice based on personal shopping trolley contents. When we are having to be disciplined by something resembling a talking lamppost and a supermarket, we should stop and wonder why we cannot discipline ourselves.

It is no coincidence that there are complaints of Britain turning into a 'nanny state' with increased rules and regulations, but maybe we get what we deserve. If we were able to set our own boundaries, then we wouldn't need lampposts in British high streets to speak to tell us to pick up our rubbish nor thousands of speed cameras on the roadways to stop us doing what we know would be safer.

Example

I was visiting a new building for a large company, with a group of people whose average age was around 50. Before we were allowed upstairs, we were told that we must hold on to the handrail when using the staircase. The person informing us told us that if we did not and were observed, we could get told off. Most of us were too speechless to comment. At the staircase, there were signs and little pictures to explain how to hold the handrail.

A little later one of the managers, who knew I was writing a book, asked what I was writing about: I explained it was about emotional immaturity, and why adults sometimes behave like children. She laughed and said that it could be written about her workplace. I was not surprised. If you treat adults like children, sometimes they will behave like children.

Using that premise, then, we should look at our own out-of-control thinking that may lead us to behaviours that are unhelpful, and consider how we could discipline ourselves.

Personal experience

My personal favourite is distraction technique, as adapted from Joy's previously mentioned brain game with Leo: it suits my butterfly mind.

If the emotional brain is hijacking logical thought and I am about to lose control in some way, I have found that the ability to force the brain away from the rising emotion to a calmer state of mind can be used in a multitude of situations. It only needs 20–30 seconds. Here are some examples.

1. Sitting in traffic jams, I have added up the numbers on number plates.

2. Walking to a difficult meeting and feeling my heart start to pound, I spelled shop signs and street names backwards under my breath.

3. Sitting in church at a funeral and about to cry copiously, I read the service sheet backwards.

Choosing music to change my mood: Vaughan Williams for relaxation, Queen for housework, Dusty Springfield for wallowing, and musicals for the 'feelgood' factor.

Music is one of the fastest mood changers, as it appears to affect the brain in interesting ways. It can be used to lift the mood and lower it too.

"Music is the shorthand of emotion"

Leo Tolstoy.

The lower the arousal, the quicker the distraction will work. In the aforementioned funeral, I was already crying, so it took a little longer. I ended up spelling the service sheet backwards slowly.

I also find it interesting when I choose not to use any techniques because I want to be aroused. We self-sabotage, even self-harm. (I can easily reduce myself to tears on purpose, with my choice of music.)

This is a powerful illustration of the distraction technique.

Illustration

Harry was a middle-aged man. He reported that he had been in an abusive relationship with his partner. The relationship had finished, but he was feeling obsessed by the memory of his ex-partner and wanted to deal with the problem of his obsessive thoughts. Over the course of the session I explained about the workings of the brain. He looked in amazement at me, and told me that something he had experienced was explained now.

Harry had physically abused his partner several times. They had decided that if it should ever happen again, his partner would ring the police. Of course, he had promised in his lucid moments that he would not lose control again – and meant it. (Most people who abuse and have addiction problems behave like this – it is called the 'cycle of abuse'.)

Unfortunately and inevitably, it happened again. His partner rang the police, but when they answered, the partner was too traumatised to speak. Harry had to take the phone and give directions to the house where they lived, which was in a remote part of the countryside. It took a few minutes to give complicated directions, and when Harry came off the phone, he was completely calm and totally horrified at what he had done. Having previously been in a complete rage, his partner could not believe the change, and called him a 'psychopath'.

Harry had been bewildered and concerned at his 'sudden' change of mood until I explained the distraction technique. In giving directions to the police, he had been forced to switch brain hemispheres, and his emotional arousal levels had fallen automatically.

Reflection

Some people respond well to the idea of 'parenting' themselves. For example, Tim, a 40-year-old man, who felt out of control in his life and was distressed, realised that he had never used any self-discipline; he had only waited for others to draw the line in his behaviour, and then reacted angrily. I asked him how his father had disciplined him, and he told me that he would say, "Enough is enough" or "You don't know when to stop". I suggested that he should start to use that language to himself if he wanted things to change. It was a revelation.

The idea works well for many people, and we can use self-dialogue such as "Come on now, you've gone far enough". However, sometimes we may have no helpful parental role model, and self-parenting may not be a concept that is easily understood. If this is the case, then we need to find exactly what sort of self-discipline works. Perhaps we need several different selves to help us through life, depending on the circumstances. Here, we are talking about different ego states to set our own boundaries:

- A parent self who tells us that we don't know when to stop.
- A nurse self who suggests that we take better care of ourselves.
- A teacher or coach self who inspires and motivates us.
- A friend self who encourages us when the going gets tough.
- A manager self who helps us problem-solve.
- A law enforcer self that tells us we have gone too far.

Personal experience

A dip in my usual cheerfulness led me back to bed one morning for a 'duvet day': this is probably the most common place to find anyone seeking some comfort away from the hassles of life. My self-dialogue was between the child in one ear telling me to stay in bed, wanting all the problems to go away, while the adult in the other ear was telling me to get a grip on myself, and that managing the situation would have to be done by me, not by staying in bed. I reminded myself of a previous time when I had felt like this, and how I had dealt with it. Eventually, after 30 minutes the adult won the argument. I got up, took control and made some life-changing decisions.

So, look at your own life, and consider times when self-discipline could help. Perhaps you are doing, or thinking of doing, something unhealthy, illegal, unhelpful or trouble-making for others. The action you take is yours, so the consequences will be yours too. Set your own boundaries, and feel in control.

Chapter 9

'Look at me... me, me, me!': the need for attention

I broke things to get attention.

Daniel Day-Lewis

❛❛It's just attention-seeking behaviour." How often do we hear that expression or use it ourselves? Children need attention. They need to give it and receive it. Problems arise when the child's needs cannot be attended to satisfactorily.

Similarly, adults *need* attention. They also need to give and receive it – in a healthy way. If someone says of an adult's behaviour, "They're just attention-seeking", it would suggest to me that the adult has not learned a more mature way of behaving.

A great many comedians report that they liked the attention they received as a child when they were the class clown. Many children use humour to deflect some unwanted attention. Babies learn very quickly how to get attention: they cry. Without the ability to communicate their needs, they would die of neglect.

Toddlers learn that they often have to compete with someone or something else for their parent's or carer's attention, and this covers all levels of society.

Example

I was sitting outside a cafe in a town centre. A family arrived: mum, dad, little boy and toddler in a pushchair. The pushchair hood contained a collection of half-consumed fizzy drinks and sweets. The dad and son went inside to order a cooked breakfast. The son ran out with a chocolate bar and a big lolly off the shelf, saying he wanted them. He was allowed to keep and eat both, while happily climbing all over a sculpture nearby.

Breakfast came and he was threatened with "going home" if he didn't come to the table. He did, but didn't want the food ordered. The half-chewed lolly was discarded. He went back to the sculpture, and there were more "going home" threats. He found the sweet wrappers in the hood of the pushchair and threw them on the ground. The parents didn't notice.

Over 30 minutes the only conversation that the mother had with her son was of a "Don't do that!" "Stop it!" nature – there was not one positive comment or observational conversation. At no time did she talk with the little girl in the pushchair, who just grunted through her dummy for sweets.

My heart went out to the little boy, who may well end up in trouble at school. Will it be his fault? There may be some people who that say that it is not the parents' fault either, as they are doing their best. However, where is the personal responsibility?

Mobile phones don't help either. I take my grandchildren to a local park near their home, which is popular with children being cared for by au pairs and nannies. It is good for the children to be able to run off and play imaginary games; it is not so good if the child is asking to be lifted up on to a piece of play equipment and is not heard. Another example is front-facing pushchairs: I dislike them intensely. I know that they were designed for convenience, but they are useless in giving the baby or child attention. I loved interacting with my children and improving their communication skills as we walked along the road. I was giving my attention and they were receiving it – healthily.

One of the main times when young children do face their parent or carer is in a supermarket: however, it tends to be such a stressful place, and the parents so time-limited, that the child is regarded as a nuisance that must be kept occupied while the shopping is done – hence the "gimme, gimme, gimme" behaviour often observed. It is not their fault at all.

Personal experience

I was a childminder when my children were younger. I looked after a toddler, Stuart, for a couple of years. It was quite normal for me to take him to the supermarket when I was doing a weekly shop, and he was never a problem.

One day, his mother asked me to look after Stuart while she went shopping: she was an intelligent, busy, working mum. She couldn't cope with him and the shopping too. She recounted a previous shopping trip:

> I gave Stuart a biscuit and he threw it on the ground. I gave him another one and he did it again. Then I gave him a cake, which he also threw away. He wasn't even happy when I bought him a little car.

> This was the same child, and the same supermarket. The difference? I didn't give him anything except my attention and I wasn't hindered by 'working parents' guilt'.

Negative attention-seeking behaviour

Certainly, being withdrawn and sulking can be a big game player in relationships. Some of my colleagues have argued with me as to whether an adult can become a child and shrink, 'Alice in Wonderland' style; however, curling up in a foetal position, sucking clothing or a thumb or pouting is not uncommon. The tonality of voice can change too. It is all attention-seeking behaviour learned a long time ago.

In some relationships the dynamic between people supports behaviour like this, and so encourages it. Provided that the people involved are both happy with the situation, then there is nothing wrong in it. However, in abusive relationships such behaviour is manipulative and, by definition, immature.

Sickness is a big attention-receiver. Most adults have experienced a time in childhood when they were sick and received attention. Emotionally immature adults have been known to use illness, whether real or imagined, to receive attention. For example, Munchausen's syndrome is this behaviour taken to the extreme, where a person feigns illness; Munchausen's syndrome by proxy is even worse, where a person will fabricate illness in another person (generally a child), or even make them ill, in order to receive attention.

What happens when a person with a genuine illness starts to cry wolf and carries on doing it all their lives? The behaviour is attention-seeking, but generally tolerated out of guilt from the attention-giver, in case it is actually for real this time. That's emotional blackmail.

The importance of boundaries

We need boundaries. At first these boundaries need to be set by our carers, then we need to set them ourselves. We will seek attention naturally in some way, and as we grow up we need to work out ourselves what attention-seeking behaviours are helpful and unhelpful.

Humans, animals and birds are kept close to their parents or carers for their own safekeeping, but gradually the boundaries are moved. In the animal kingdom it can happen quite quickly, and fledgling birds are encouraged out of their nest in weeks. This is not so with humans, but the boundaries must be moved otherwise the child will not grow up healthily. We can see in the animal kingdom that the old ways of keeping animals in zoos, in too small an enclosure, could send them mad. On the other hand, leaving newborn lambs in unfenced fields would lead to losses.

There are sheep in the fields near my home. I watch the antics of newborn lambs with a smile. They appear to be literally full of the joys of spring. I also notice that as they get a little bigger, they start to explore their boundaries: if there is a gap in the hedge or fence, they will find it. Freedom! However, it is at a price, if they are near a road and not found before it is too late.

I know as a parent that it is nerve-wracking to let your children out of your sight for the first time. The first time to a shop, to school on their own, the first bus or train trip, the first holiday – but if we don't widen their boundaries and let them go, we are not encouraging healthy emotional or intellectual growth. Needless to say, the opposite situation – letting children have free will all the time – can be harmful to their future growth. No parent can get it totally right, and in families it is not always easy to allow for the individuality of each child. The variety of characteristics and personalities that two people can produce is a miracle. Communication, compromise and negotiation are the key elements.

Personal experience

I recall a school trip to the seaside: I would have been about eight years old. I purposely walked off the beach and got lost. I can recall wanting to feel special, and not one of the masses. I can certainly recognise that I was attention-seeking.

As an outgoing person, tall too, I tend to stand out physically in a crowd. I discovered that an easy way to get personal attention was to become withdrawn and sit quietly; I can remember doing that as a teenager. It didn't work at home, but it did at school. Although I seem to remember that it didn't last long, the real me would burst out.

As an adult I developed another way of receiving attention, one that still works, but perhaps in a healthy way. I wasn't the class clown, but I made myself pick up spiders! I only started doing it to be different from everyone else. I didn't like it particularly, but I could see that it would have its uses. This has turned out to be a most useful behaviour, as I live in the country and spiders hide in all sorts of nooks and crannies.

At the time I was training to be a nursery nurse, I had a boyfriend and his family owned a dog, a labrador called Bruno. I would have loved to own a dog, but due to family circumstances this was not possible. Bruno was left on his own all day and allowed to bark; also, he was undisciplined when the family was around. I did what came naturally and set boundaries, as I found Bruno's misbehaviour irritating. I would give Bruno loving attention, but use a firm voice and not tolerate any nonsense. It amused me when the whole family were watching TV in the evening, and Bruno would come and rest his head in my lap. It happened whenever I visited. I didn't understand why he was responding to me until later.

Illustration

We like children asking questions. In fact, we encourage it – although under-fives do seem to have the question "Why?' on a constant loop at times.

However, what about a woman married to a man who is driving her to distraction by continually asking questions? It was the man who came to see me. Steven could see that his questioning could become irritating, but didn't know how to stop, or even why he did it. The problem was worse when they were going anywhere. Steven would ask all about the destination. He said he wanted to express interest, but his wife was despairing of the interrogation: one or two answers were never enough.

A little information-gathering led to the following revelation. Steven was the middle child in a family, jostling for attention. One day, the family was on a car journey when Steven asked a question: he was about eight or nine years old. Steven's father commented on the excellence of the question. He remembered feeling good: he felt proud that his dad had approved of his question. He decided to ask more questions in other situations. "I would wait until my mother was busy in the kitchen, and then ask her questions."

Steven had found a way to have his need for attention met. The problem was that while he had grown up, married and was performing well in the workplace, he had not learned to stop asking questions. That part of his brain was stuck in the feeling that he got as a child, which was taking over the adult. When it was suggested that Steven could stop being the little boy, he didn't mind in the slightest – it made complete sense. He was more than happy to stop thinking up questions to ask all the time. I hope he still is.

Relationships

Observations suggest to me that attention needs in adult relationships work mainly from variations of one of the three following models.

Adult and adult

Two adults are able to relate to each other as adults. They explore and support getting their individual adult needs met within the relationship. Intellectually there may be a difference in IQ, but their EQs (emotional intelligence) are well matched. They can enjoy moments of childlike fun together. There may be instances of childish behaviour, but these are not a dominant feature of the relationship; neither are they tolerated to any great extent. Boundaries are drawn and kept to: there is necessarily some dependence, but overall they retain their own independence. These are healthy relationships where communication is open and effective. When the going gets tough, they are able to problem-solve and support each other.

Adult and adult mini-me

Two adults start out on an equal footing, but at certain times one of the adults begins to display a significant amount of childish behaviour: for example, sulks and tantrums. The relationship changes into one between an adult and an adult mini-me. Communication can break down.

If the change in the dynamic is supported and encouraged by the adult, this relationship can survive and even thrive. A dependency can be created, but it suits the needs of the individuals. This may not be to everyone's taste, but if it is not upsetting anyone and the people concerned are happy, then that is okay.

However, if this change in dynamic is not supported by the adult, it can lead to a breakdown in the relationship. The adult has lost an equal, and the adult mini-me cannot find what they are looking for; moreover, the adult can find living or working with the adult mini-me draining and unfulfilling. Over time they will become frustrated and resentful, while the adult mini-me also becomes angry and upset because the adult cannot solve their problems. This can become an extremely unhappy and destructive relationship that could be sustained for years.

Two adult mini-mes

These are two adults who cannot communicate as adults, and both are attempting to resolve their childhood needs instead of their adult ones. This relationship has a high degree of unhappiness, as each partner cannot provide what the other is seeking – it can even become chaotic. They may have good, even high, IQs and be highly competent in the workplace, but emotionally they are on average eight years old and under. Imagine two eight-year-olds attempting to live or work together and organising anything: one can understand the difficulties that arise as a result.

Reflection

The 'eureka' moments in therapeutic situations are particularly joyful. I hope that this book will provide readers with their own moments of personal revelation – moments that could change their lives, and those around them, for the better.

Is there any personal behaviour that you can think of that gets you attention, but by means that might be considered childish?

Do you need to change the behaviour?

Is the behaviour causing you problems?

Is the behaviour causing other people problems?

Do you want to change that behaviour?

Can you recall when you first started using that behaviour, and why?

Do you still need to behave like that now?

Chapter 10

'I'm sad': grief and loss

Even a happy life cannot be without a measure of darkness, and the word happy would lose its meaning if it were not balanced by sadness. It is far better to take things as they come along with patience and equanimity.

Carl Jung

A sad child is hard to resist. Tears, sobs or just a downcast look can attract attention. We want to make it better. A well-known soother is "Have a sweet to make it better". More often than not, it is a way to stop the child making a scene. Listen to the message the child is getting: "I'm hurting. It's painful. I've made a fuss. I'm being offered a treat or reward as compensation." It does not take long for the child to learn that pain equals gain. It may only be material gain, but they are not to know that material gain often has a short shelf-life.

Over the years I have come to understand my own psychology. However, it still doesn't stop me, as soon as I am feeling sad, fed up or thwarted in some way, from going straight to the cupboard and looking for something sweet: "I deserve it", I can hear mini-me saying. My memory-matches take me back to illness and hot Ribena and digestive biscuits. Many adults may do the same with alcohol, and generally they were not offered a drink as a child. Nonetheless, to hear the language used by adults, alcohol is treated like a reward for something painful: an awful day at work, the screaming children, a feeling of inadequacy, feeling isolated.

As children we are not always taught to tolerate the painful things in life. I am not talking about criminal abuse here – I am talking about the interactions and events in life that make us sad.

Understanding sadness and grief

Sadness is part of a normal life, and children should be taught how to tolerate and manage it. Bad and sad things will happen. Adults cannot prevent them from happening, although they would love to protect their child from all the ills of the world. It is not realistic. Especially when it comes to exam results and their consequenses.

When I was a teenager I was amazed to see a friend, Emma, being bought presents any time anything sad, difficult or unpleasant happened to her – by this I mean the normal downs of life. Every time, her mother bought her a present: it was expected. However, this became a problem as Emma grew up and married. She found it difficult to cope with the perfectly normal ups and downs of domestic living. The ups were okay, but her partner did not reward her every time there was a domestic crisis: he just got on with problem-solving, while Emma was having a tantrum or sulk with no reward.

The grieving process

There is an expression, 'mad with grief', and there is no doubt that any prolonged extreme emotion can leave the mind unbalanced. Sadness is an emotion that can be felt for longer than some others. There are no rules for how long the grieving process can take. Some people loathe the use of the word 'process', but that is what it is: a series of brain actions. The brain processes emotions and, in doing so, places the emotions in different parts of the brain, as the mind works through the different stages of the process. Otherwise, certain parts of the brain become as overloaded as a filing cabinet if we tried to file too much in it.

Usually, the process will follow an order of: shock → disbelief → denial → anger → acceptance. There is no set timing for how long this process can take, and all these stages are totally normal. The whys and wherefores of grief are personal, and the reason we give to terrible events happening lies with our own belief system. However, the brain has evolved to allow for terrible events to occur, and for memories to move slowly to a different place in the brain where they are not so painful. Then normal functioning can resume. It is when the process appears to get stuck after a length of time, that it can be helpful to seek advice.

I can certainly recognise all these stages in my own life in relation to the death of friends, the loss of a job and loss of personal integrity. The stages lasted different lengths of time for different life events. When should grief (the 'Bereavement Exclusion') be medicalised and treated with medication? The new DSM-5 (Diagnostic and Statistical Manual of Mental Disorders) suggests two months, but that could be considered too soon by some people.

Removal of the bereavement exclusion

The bereavement exclusion in DSM-4, which has been removed in DSM-5, was intended to exclude individuals experiencing depressive symptoms lasting less than two months after the death of a loved one from a diagnosis of MDD. The new edition characterises bereavement as a severe psychological stressor that can incite a major depressive episode, even shortly after the loss of a loved one.

The implications

As detractors have pointed out, this contentious revision risks pathologising a normal human process, grief. Individuals may be diagnosed with depression even in the absence of severe depression symptoms (i.e., suicidal ideation) and even though their symptoms may be transient. Furthermore, in a recent article in *World Psychiatry*, Drs. Jerome Wakefield and Michael First call into question the validity of research supporting removing the exclusion, concluding, '...there is no scientific basis for removing the bereavement exclusion from the DSM-5.'

Medscape Psychiatry – A Guide to DSM-5

The journalist, Johann Hari, wrote some years ago about the merits of anti –depressants (see Further Reading Bibliography). Then a couple of years later, he realised that while he was missing the lows, he was also missing the highs. He weaned himself off them (warning: never go 'cold turkey' from anti-depressants – it can be harmful and dangerous). He wrote that, meanwhile, his friend continued to take them. His friend had started taking them because he was sad at not having a girlfriend. Now he wasn't sad anymore – he just sat in the pub, not caring that he didn't have a girlfriend.

I certainly would agree with the accepted advice given that no one should make major life decisions until at least six months after an upsetting life event. There are any number of stories from people who made big decisions too quickly when they were still unable to think logically, and then regretted it in the cold light of day when rational, logical thinking re-entered their lives.

Loss

A large amount of personal sadness arises from a sense of personal loss. Most people associate grief with the loss of a person, but the loss of anything should not be underestimated: for example, the loss of a job, pet, home, relationship, youth and even one's own abilities.

Losing a family member is generally the most emotionally painful experience that a person can have. We should never underestimate an individual's grief, as we do not know their personal story. Each child is different: their sadness should be tolerated and understood, but not endlessly rewarded. As a therapist, I saw many adults still grieving for a grandparent who had died when they were still a child or teenager.

The emotion of sadness is often explained as "feeling down" or "feeling depressed". People talk about self-medicating: this means not bothering the doctor and using alcohol or other mind-altering substances, even self-harming activities. Anti-depressants can help some people, some of the time. In August 2013, the Health and Social Care Information Centre published data showing that more than 50 million prescriptions for anti-depressants were issued in 2012, the highest ever number and 7.5% up on the year before. I feel we should be careful. As the bereavement exclusion has been removed in DSM-5, these figures are likely to rise again. We now have at least two, if not three, generations growing up believing that sadness should not be tolerated, but rewarded or medicated in some way. I don't believe that this is healthy. Grief and loss hurt and hurt badly, but it is a normal part of life that needs managing rather than medicating.

Emotional triggers

As adults we can suddenly become emotionally taken over by sadness. It can be triggered by anything. Sometimes it is something obvious: for example, photographs or a sound. Music can bring about a sudden change of mood, but feeling an overwhelming sadness in the middle of the supermarket, when a certain song is played over the tannoy, is not helpful. Both photographs and music can whisk our minds back decades very quickly to past times. Happy times that have gone equal loss, while sad times can also equal loss. Often it is a bittersweet mixture of both happy and sad feelings. I was sad attending a friend's funeral, but happy to meet up again with some old work colleagues.

The death of Princess Diana in 1997 affected thousands of people emotionally. Were they all crying for Diana? No – however, journalists were reporting that, although they and others felt little about Diana, they were crying and did not know why. No one person would have had the same reason as another but in all of them, the images and sounds would have memory-matched something special in their own lives, and they were hijacked by the emotion.

How, as a therapist, can I tell quite quickly how emotionally aroused a person might be about a past life event? If the event has been filed by the brain to a place of acceptance, it is highly likely that the person in front of me can tell me about that event, maybe even a horrific event, as if they are telling me a story. This is called narrative memory, and can be retold with little or no emotion. If someone is telling me about a life event but becoming emotional at the same time, it is likely that the memory is still stuck somewhere else, and the person is still reliving the event. This is what happens in post-traumatic stress disorder (PTSD; see Chapter 11).

Personal experience

Like most people's lives, there have been painful events in mine. I know the memories are filed away in the right place, because I can retell personal life events in a narrative way without becoming emotionally aroused. I also know that I can cry about losses and provoke and pick at those memories if I want to indulge in some self-pity. Most actors, when asked how they can cry on demand, will say they just remember a sad life event. I also know that I can be taken unawares, tears pricking my eyes, and then recognise that some emotion has been memory-matched in some way. It is not always obvious although, being me, I analyse why. For example, In the 1990s I was happily married and living in a big city, quite near some schools. My children were in their twenties and away from home. I noticed on a Saturday morning that a coach would draw up outside, and children would get on board with a selection of musical instruments. On looking at them, the tears would well up. I could not understand why at first, and then remembered the many years of taking my children to orchestra and choir practice and listening to concerts. I was grieving for the loss of my children as youngsters, and for the loss of family life. I can still 'go there' at Christmas time, especially listening to choirs.

Illustration

Marcus Trescothick. Not an easy name to say, but one that I was able to use to my advantage in 2005. The cricket series, The Ashes, was drawing to a thrilling close and I was listening to BBC Radio 5 on a headset while shopping. The presenter, Simon Mayo, asked for any advice on how to keep calm. Nothing was forthcoming and he asked again. Despite being in the middle of a supermarket, I contacted the show. I was put on the live radio programme, stressful in itself. Simon Mayo was somewhat surprised when I suggested a breathing exercise. Sounding cynical, he asked me to explain. To make it sound more attractive for radio, I added a distraction technique using Trescothick's name. Simon thanked me, but I could tell that he didn't think much of the suggestion. Imagine my pleasure when about five minutes later, one of his colleagues excitedly exclaimed, "Hey that breathing thing, it works! I'm going down to the England dressing room to tell them." Result!

In 2006, Marcus Trescothick hit the headlines for something else. He had to return from an overseas tour with a virus, but there were rumours that it was actually something else. It turned out not to be a virus, but a serious episode of depression. By 2006, I was formulating my ideas about emotional maturity and was interested in the background to the story. I waited to read somewhere that some childhood memory had been triggered. I felt it was inevitable. The background story was not made public for a while, but when it came out, there was what I had been waiting for: going on an overseas tour had reminded the adult Marcus of a horrible time and overwhelming misery he had felt when he was ten years old and sent away to school. What exactly were the particular triggers in 2006? After all, he had toured for many years before then. Could having had a baby in 2005, a child of his own, be a clue? In 2008, Marcus published his autobiography, *Coming Back To Me*. He wrote that his bouts of depression were triggered by separation (loss and grief) from his wife and young daughters.

As Marcus had grown up, the little boy grew up to be a world class cricketer. The cricket skills did not stay as those of a ten-year-old; neither did his body, as he grew into a man. However, a small part of his emotional brain was stuck in a state of fear at ten years old. The frightened emotion of that time would have been imprinted on his immature brain, and his brain wanted to protect him from feeling like that again.

I believe that the problem could be solved for good. Talking therapy? Yes, maybe, but the correct talking therapy. A therapy that de-traumatises that hijacking emotion. One that focuses on allowing adult Marcus to reassure the frightened little boy Marcus, and leave him behind where he belongs – in the last century, in 1986 – not to keep hijacking the present and future.

A warning

I was on a training course for a local support group. There were around 20 mostly middle-aged people. A local support group leader from another group took a session. We were asked to think of a secret, something so secret that we had not told anyone. Whoah! I thought: red light – do not go there. So I didn't. I watched while others wrote theirs on a piece of paper that was torn up at the end of the exercise. We were then asked to empathise with victims with secrets. At the end, almost as a throwaway, it was announced that if anyone had been disturbed by the exercise, then they should speak to someone. If, I thought – if? Inside I was incandescent at something I considered to be abusive. The trainers were responsible people but were completely unaware of trauma and brain function.

Reflection

Barbara came to see me with her eight-year-old son, Danny. She had talked to me before the visit about her concerns that Danny still had a problem with outbursts of anger, five years after his father had left home. From the conversation, I guessed what might be happening. I chatted to Danny and it was mentioned that he and his mum had played a game of snakes and ladders the evening before. I took my chance. I gently observed that life was like a game of snakes and ladders. Some days it is all ladders, some days mostly snakes, some days a mixture, and some days neither of them. However, we have to keep throwing the dice and move forwards, we cannot go back and undo our throw of the dice. Danny got it immediately.

Barbara admitted later that with the best will in the world, she had been trying to make the child's life one of all ladders, rather than snakes. That is what I had guessed.

How do you deal with the snakes in life?

Do you feel that life should be all ladders?

Do you give yourself another shake of the dice and move on?

Chapter 11

'I'm frightened': fear

The world is full of frightened children.

Kurt Vonnegut

It is my belief that this chapter informs all the other chapters. Fear is what is at the root of 'chasing rainbows' behaviour.

I believe that some adults experience a sense of fear of 'not being good enough' in certain areas of their life. The root of the fear lies in childhood, when they were first able to feel that they were not good enough in some way. It may result from something actual or something perceived; there was a level of trauma associated with the experience or experiences, and the brain still has the ability to switch on the fear alarm.

"I'm frightened" is a perfectly normal and healthy reaction to a situation where we feel under threat. We experience a feeling of fear: it could come suddenly or creep up more slowly. Our bodies may show psychological changes, including breathing increasingly rapidly, a heart rate increase and a feeling of nausea. Our bodies are responding normally and telling us to take action using one of the most primitive resources we have: the flight, flight or freeze response.

Post-traumatic stress disorder

Many people have heard of post-traumatic stress disorder (PTSD) – it is mostly spoken of and written about in realation to the armed forces, but it can affect anyone, and few will know the diagnostic criteria. PTSD is the development of characteristic and persistent symptoms, along with difficulty functioning, after exposure to a life or integrity-threatening experience, or an event that either involves a threat to life, integrity or serious injury. In some cases the symptoms of PTSD disappear with time, as the brain processes or files the memories in another part of the brain, whereas in other cases they persist for many years. Why this happens has a great deal to do with the person getting other needs met healthily.

The following is an accepted description of PTSD. The symptoms can arise suddenly, gradually or come and go over time. Sometimes symptoms appear seemingly out of the blue; at other times, they are triggered by something that reminds the person of the original traumatic event, such as a noise, image, certain words or a smell. While everyone experiences PTSD differently, there are three main types of symptoms. These are required for the diagnosis of PTSD, and may be divided into clusters of symptoms: they should be present for at least one month.

1. Re-experiencing the traumatic event:

- Intrusive, upsetting memories of the event.
- Flashbacks – acting or feeling like the event is happening again.
- Nightmares – either of the event, or of other frightening things.
- Feelings of intense distress when reminded of the trauma.
- Intense physical reactions to reminders of the event – for example, a pounding heart, rapid breathing, nausea, muscle tension, sweating.

2. Avoidance and emotional numbing:

- Avoiding activities, places, thoughts or feelings that remind the person of the trauma.
- Inability to remember important aspects of the trauma.
- Loss of interest in activities and life in general.
- Feeling detached from others and emotionally numb.
- Sense of a limited future – for example, not expecting to live a normal life span, get married, have a career.

3. Increased arousal:

- Difficulty falling or staying asleep.
- Irritability or outbursts of anger.
- Difficulty concentrating.
- Hypervigilance – feeling on constant 'red alert'.
- Feeling jumpy and easily startled.

Other common symptoms of PTSD are:

- anger and irritability
- guilt, shame or self-blame
- substance abuse
- depression and hopelessness
- suicidal thoughts and feelings
- feeling alienated and alone
- feelings of mistrust and betrayal
- headaches, stomach problems, chest pain

PTSD is a major psychological illness. It causes a great deal of distress to the person experiencing it and their family – especially if it has not been diagnosed, which often happens with personnel from the armed forces and the emergency services.

The list of symptoms and behaviour make interesting reading. While full-blown PTSD is dramatic and obvious, what about a milder form of the symptoms, something that could be called 'low-level PTSD', 'sub-threshold PTSD' or 'frozen trauma'? It appeared to me that over the years of helping and supporting people, I was observing people who showed various degrees of reactions to trauma. It could be 100% PTSD developed from exposure to a very frightening or threatening event, or similar symptoms arising from a lower level of exposure to something that the person found frightening. It may have been real or perceived.

Following this train of thought, I wondered if some of the behaviour that I was observing was in fact that of a traumatised child. If obvious symptoms of PTSD can go unrecognised in adults, then how much more difficult would it be to recognise a frightened mini-me taking over an adult's brain?

Extreme fear is the common emotion

If PTSD can go unrecognised and undiagnosed, then what about one of the symptoms – panic attacks? They can be misdiagnosed as a symptom of physical ill-health rather than emotional imbalance. A GP, Suzanne, came to see me with recognisable symptoms of PTSD, but she was undergoing investigations for a heart problem. This is not uncommon. I mentioned to Suzanne that I was aware of many people with misdiagnosed and unrecognised panic attacks, and why weren't doctors able to diagnose them? She told me that if patients were told their symptoms were panic attacks, then there might be a possibility of missing a heart problem.

If you have ever experienced PTSD or known someone that does, the diagnostic criteria listed above may be familiar to you. However, look at the criteria again and think about a behaviour that you may have. Maybe a phobia? Maybe an overreaction to something or somebody? Perhaps an avoidance behaviour of some sort? You are unlikely to be experiencing full-blown PTSD, but what about a 'low-level trauma', a 'sub-threshold trauma' or 'frozen trauma'? For example, many people will have a strong reaction to their school uniform colour, avoiding it at all costs in their life and in all manner of objects, even decades later.

Phobias are built on these foundations: this is why so many people think that their fears will be judged as illogical by others – because generally, they are. The fear is real, but in the majority of cases it will be built on an emotional memory-match that has become distorted in time and something 'like' the original incident will trigger the memory-match and associated feelings. The past has become mixed up with the present. Personally, I found phobias fascinating to work with. It can be like the childhood game of 'pass the parcel'. As each layer is removed something else is revealed, until the original memory-match is discovered.

Scarred for life?

So, is that it – is this fear for life? Not so: as I mentioned previously, the symptoms may go away, or they may not develop fully. Hundreds of people may experience a similar horrifying event, such as a train crash or bomb explosion. Some people will develop PTSD, while others will not. Why is this? The whole of the person's life needs to be looked at: those people getting their needs met in a healthy way are less likely to develop PTSD.

Example

Sue developed PTSD mainly due to the legal process after a bomb attack. Years of continually retelling and reliving the events led to the memories becoming toxic. The continual emphasis was on everything she had lost and could not do anymore, due to the injuries to her legs.

I once worked on an acute psychiatric unit. There was an ex-serviceman with PTSD in the unit: he was terrified, and medicated. He was encouraged to attend a group relaxation session, and lay on the floor with the others. The session leader put on some soothing background music. She started to ask people to imagine themselves in a restful place: "Imagine a green field..." The man shot up, shaking like a leaf, and ran out of the room. It transpired that he had served in Bosnia, and had been blown up by a landmine in a field.

This incident strongly highlights the need for individually tailored help. For example, I used relaxation techniques as a part of therapy, but understood that a 'one size fits all' script would not work for everyone. I used the client's own suggestions for visualisations and was permissive with the language used, not prescriptive. The client's memory-matches to my words were unknown and could contribute to resistance.

Sub-threshold trauma

As a therapist I became increasingly interested in this low-level, sub-threshold or frozen trauma. I believed that I was observing evidence of this kind of trauma in a great many clients. For example, something happens to a person in childhood. They feel in danger, or at least frightened. It might be a physical threat or an emotional threat. It may be real. It may just be perceived, but no less of a threat (a child's brain doesn't see the bigger picture). As they mature, they grow up physically, intellectually and chronologically – but emotionally? Are they stuck sometimes? Are there certain 'buttons' that can be pressed, which cause the emotional brain to regress and behave as if the 'fight, flight or freeze' reaction has been activated? Could they be 'frozen in time'? I believe so.

Kenny Logan is a retired footballer. Like several retired sportspeople, he has appeared on a TV reality shows: this one was *Strictly Come Dancing*. Ten minutes into his first day he was struck with a real and unexpected terror. Ola, the professional dancer, was teaching him some basic steps:

"And I mean basic," he says. She asked him to clap to the beat. He did not have a clue what she meant. Suddenly, he tells me, he was transported back to being a ten-year-old dyslexic kid, floundering at school because not only did the words on the page not mean anything, but he couldn't even recognise them as words.

"It was horrible," he recalls. "I hadn't felt that sort of thing for years and years. I knew I couldn't do what was being asked of me, and I wanted to walk out of there rather than make an idiot of myself trying." (*Daily Mail*, 1 December 2007)

Another reality show is *Big Brother* and its companion, *Celebrity Big Brother*. Again, both endlessly fascinating for someone with an interest in human behaviour. Many years ago, the TV and radio personality, Vanessa Feltz, appeared as a contestant. She is a highly educated, erudite and intelligent person. The time came for her to be ejected, which she took badly. This rejection by her peers came not long after her husband had left her and her mother had died. She became highly emotional, found a piece of chalk and wrote a multitude words all over a table top. The words were all linked with loss and rejection. It looked as if she had 'lost the plot', which momentarily she had: she had become 'mad with grief'. It made gripping television, but was very sad too. My heart went out to her. Sometimes TV companies purposely choose celebrities who are emotionally vulnerable because it makes good TV.

Personal experience

My first memories are from around two and half to three years old. I don't believe they are false memories, as I have always remembered these little snapshots of life without the aid of someone else's narrative or photographic proof. They can be dated because of the age of my sister in the memories and my grandfather's death.

A recent TV series called *Call the Midwife* brought back very strong memories of being taken to the children's clinic and watching my sister being weighed on some scales, just like the ones on the programme. I had to stand in my vest. As mentioned in the introduction, I also recall being left in a nursery with my sister, because my mother had to go away. I will acknowledge that I was left twice and the memories are probably mixed up. I don't remember anything particularly unpleasant.

Roll the years on to 17 and the careers mistress at school. What to do with me? I liked working with younger children and often was sent to a junior school to help out. So, a nursery nursing course was suggested to me: the number one college was Norlands, in Chislehurst, Kent. I was adamant that I was not going to Norlands. The school and my mother could not understand my protests. So, I ended up in Windsor and the whole course of my life changed – all because of a 14-year-old memory-match.

I certainly don't need to go back into the memory. If I have 'forgotten' something unpleasant, other than being left, then I will leave it hidden. I have no need to pick at old wounds and make a forgotten memory a toxic one.

What I find endlessly fascinating is that bad memories do not necessarily mean running away from that experience. I was in hospital at seven and it wasn't all good – but that was when I decided I wanted to become a nurse. I loved working on the maternity units and, years later, walking on to a psychiatric unit as an agency nursery nurse in 1995, I immediately felt at home. From the age of around 11 years, I used to go, on occasion, into the office with my mother who worked as a personal assistant. They were great days out in central London with pleasant people, and there was fun to be had filing and playing with the typewriters. I vowed that I never wanted to work in an office. I don't know why, but I kept to that one, too.

Memory-matching and post-traumatic stress disorder

Memory-matching plays a large part in PTSD and any variations of it. A friend, Sarah, suddenly married her long-time partner, and I rang to give her my good wishes. She explained that she had been due to undergo a brain operation, and she and her partner thought that they should legalise matters beforehand. I was shocked, and asked her what happened. She told me that she had gone for an eye test and the optician mentioned that there was some age-related deterioration in one eye – the word 'blindness' was mentioned. Going blind had always been Sarah's greatest fear in life. She left the opticians' shop, and suddenly felt very dizzy and sick. A trip to the GP revealed that she had high blood pressure and needed further investigations; there was a suggestion of a brain tumour. Sarah's parents paid for her to consult the best doctors.

The decision was made for her to undergo a brain operation; just one blood test was remaining. She got married. The blood test proved negative, and the operation was called off. I said, "Forgive me for saying, but it sounds as if you had a panic attack outside the shop?" She agreed that this was now being diagnosed. She asked me how I knew.

Illustration

Gina was driving to work and experienced a panic attack, apparently out of the blue. The next time she drove down the same road, the feelings returned. Then the feelings returned if she was nearing the road, and increased until she had to take sick leave because she was unable to drive to work. It appeared to be a simple case of matching up the memory to a road incident that she had experienced – but there wasn't one. I was puzzled. Then I asked her to pinpoint the moment that the panic attack started, and to describe what else was going on around her. I could see that a connection had been made. She told me that the car radio was playing a song that she remembers was playing on the radio at home when an ambulance had come to collect her: at the time, she was experiencing a miscarriage. It is this kind of progression of fear-inducing memory-matches that can be at the root of agoraphobia.

Reliving trauma in everyday life

Just before a workplace meeting, a colleague, Chrissie decided to make a quick visit to the cloakroom. She had used the cloakroom many times before. She returned a few minutes later, looking flustered and with a large graze down one arm. Chrissie explained that she had tried to unlock the toilet cubicle door, but the lock was stuck. She tried several times, but then panicked. She stood on the toilet, put one foot on the toilet roll holder, breaking it, and hitched herself over the partition wall. As she had slid over the other side, she had grazed her arm: fairly unbelievable.

We went back to the cloakroom. The cubicle she had used was still locked on the inside. We looked at a similar lock. It was a sliding lock. She had been trying to turn it, and in her hurry had panicked when it would not open, however many times she tried to turn it. I asked Chrissie whether she had ever experienced a similar type of episode. She told me that as a child she had got locked in a toilet on a visit to the dentist. Despite now being in her forties and an intelligent woman, she had become a frightened little girl again.

She wondered how I had guessed that something like this had probably happened before. I explained that I knew a little about the traumatised brain, and that in her panicky state she had experienced a 'flight, fight or freeze' moment and ended up doing something that now seemed a bit silly. She was going to have to explain to reception why there was a toilet cubicle door locked from the inside, and a broken toilet roll holder hanging off the wall. In Chrissie's case, emotional arousal had definitely made her temporarily 'stupid'.

I should be very surprised if any readers cannot identify a time when a simple situation has turned into something frightening, and the resulting action has not been the most sensible one in the circumstances. There may be an exact match, as in Chrissie's two cloakroom experiences. However, more often than not, it is something not quite so obvious – but the match is always there, with a little searching.

Reflection

Sometimes people know how old their hijacking 'mini-me' is, but are not clear exactly in what area of their life the missing needs are. First, it is useful to compile a list of emotional needs to complete in the present day, as an adult. Then, fill in the list as the identified 'mini-me'. In this way, you can pinpoint where the exact problem lies. Here are some areas to think about:

- security
- love and attention
- achievement
- privacy
- friendship
- personal value
- control
- meaning and purpose

The Emotional Needs Audit project has a useful website and questionnaire that can be filled in (www.enaproject. org).

If you feel that you still hold some traumatic memories, there are several therapies that can help reprocess the traumatic memory with minimal distress. For example, if you have a phobia arising from a frightening incident in childhood, the actual phobia can be dealt with effectively and quickly. However, if the phobia is attached to another unresolved and undiscovered problem, it may return.

If you believe that some reprocessing of a traumatic event could help, look for accredited practitioners of the following therapies:

- Rewind Technique
- Fast Phobia Cure
- Visual and Kinesthetic Dissociation Technique
- Neuro-Linguistic Programming (NLP) Trauma Process
- Accelerated Resolution Therapy (ART)
- Emotional Freedom Technique (EFT)
- Eye Movement Desensitisation and Reprocessing (EMDR)

Chapter 12

'It's not my fault – they did it': taking responsibility

When you blame others, you give up your power to change.
Robert Anthony

Why do we, as adults, so readily blame others for actions that we have personally taken? Because we did it as children, and have not grown up to take mature, adult responsibility. We were frightened that we would get into trouble, and so we said anything that would remove the blame from us. Did we really like ourselves then when we dumped someone else in it? It might have got us out of immediate trouble, but did it make us feel good about ourselves? Immediately, yes probably, but later on?

It is funny when we hear children saying things like "It wasn't my fault, it was his/hers" – especially when it is obvious that it wasn't. However, is this any sillier than saying "It's the government's fault"?

Here are some everyday blaming statements:

"He wouldn't get out of the bathroom."
"She didn't put the alarm on."
"It was the dog/cat/kids."

"It's not my fault, I wasn't told.", "Did you ask/listen?",
"I shouldn't have to."

Sportspeople provide endless illustrations of blaming something or someone else. A French football player, Zinedine Zidane, headbutted an Italian opponent in the chest in front of three billion people during the 2006 World Cup: he didn't get away with it, but what was his excuse? The Italian had insulted his mother. A teacher on a radio phone-in was in despair: "How can I teach my pupils to take responsibility? Every day in the playground I hear, 'He called my mum a rude name'." More recently, another footballer bit an opponent's arm. The next day, children were doing a 'Suarez' in the playground and biting other children.

I am picking on footballers because they get enormous publicity, but racing drivers, cyclists, golfers and tennis players all can behave in an immature, childish way. John McEnroe, the American tennis player, is probably still the best example of a sportsman displaying childish tantrums ever seen, and that was back in the 1970s. Footballers are not the only role models that we learn from: it is astonishing how many politicians' mistakes are the media's fault when they are found out.

When it comes to ourselves, there is a whole array of institutions to blame:

The speeding fine is the government's fault.
Our bounced cheque is the bank's fault.
Being overweight is the food manufacturer's fault.
Being late is the transport company's fault.
Getting drunk is the pub's fault.
Going to bed late is the TV company's fault.
Losing one's driving licence is the DVLC's fault.

Moreover, there are so many people to blame: family, neighbours, teachers, classmates, bosses and colleagues.

Then there is the biggest of all: the fault of birth. Parents can't win. In addition, I have heard all of the following as an explanation for present difficulties.

I was an only child/I was in a big family.
I was the youngest/middle/eldest child.
I wasn't loved/I was loved too much.
I had no freedom/I had too much freedom.
They didn't care what I did/They cared too much what I did.
My parents divorced/My parents stayed together.
I was suffocated/I was given too much independence.
I was made to go to university/I wasn't given a chance to go to university.
My mother worked/My mother stayed at home.
I was spoilt/I was neglected.
I went to an academic school/I went to a school that didn't stretch me.
I'm an Aries/I was born on a Wednesday.

So it goes on – and a picture emerges. When something happens that we do not like, we will tend to put the blame on something or someone else. Where is personal responsibility? We do not live in isolation, we touch one another in our lives. Our words and deeds are like a pebble that we drop in the water, and the ripples can go on and on – but who threw the pebble? However, there is one common factor in this scenario: the person who is blaming something or someone else is reacting to a situation where they are emotionally aroused.

Illustration

"It wasn't my fault, it was my wife's," said Pete. He was explaining why he had got drunk the night before.

"What happened?" I asked. "Well, we were watching TV in the sitting room. We had an argument, so I got up, went into the kitchen and drank the rest of the bottle of wine in the fridge. Then I went into my office and drunk some more."

"Did your wife open the bottle?" I asked. "Did she pour the wine into a glass?"

"Did she lift the glass to your mouth?"

Pete looked sheepishly at me. He had got the point.

Actions and consequences

What is a reaction? I think the word tells us: it is a repeat action. If that is so, then we are defaulting to a behaviour with history. Our brain is automatically telling us to do something that we have done before. So, "that's all right then, it's our brain's fault. We couldn't help it".

Short-term gain is all that any person with an impulsive behaviour problem can see, and this can occur at any age. As mentioned previously, I have a fascination with emotional maturity because it lies behind many of the problems presented by adults. They experience an emotional button being pressed and appear unable to control it. This is why I believe that many 'mental' health problems should really be described as 'emotional' health problems.

It is important, if using a threat or punishment with a child, to make it something that will take effect in the next few hours – no longer. Also, to make it actionable and carry it out. I know it is tempting, but how many times do you hear a parent say to a child: "If you carry on, you won't come on holiday with us!", or "You won't go to the burger bar with us". You just know that, of course, the child will go on holiday with them and they will go to the burger bar, whatever happens – the problem is that, generally, so does the child.

It is my belief that the ability to understand that actions lead to consequences comes slowly with the maturity of the emotional brain. This appears to occur at different times for different people. There is also evidence arising from published research that a male brain may mature emotionally later than a female brain. Why this is the case I have no idea, as it does not seem to be very useful.

Example

I sometimes use water and food colouring in a clear bowl to demonstrate actions and consequences in workshops. It works well with younger people who have not yet fully understood the role of actions and consequences. I fill the large bowl with water and put one drop of food colouring into it. It is quite hypnotic to watch, as the colour drops and then gently swirls around, until eventually all the water is coloured from just one drop. Then I add another colour, and we see everything change again. The ripple effect is powerful stuff. There is just one action – sometimes one small action – but the ripples go on and on.

Modelling behaviour

If, as adults, we show children that we blame others for our actions, and that it is okay for adults to behave in ways that children should not, what signals are they picking up? It can amuse (and upset) a parent to see their young child develop habits that they have picked up from a primary carer, such as sitting, walking or eating in a certain way, or repeating a well-used phrase. For example, I recall a two-year-old child in my toddler group 30 years ago, playing shops. When I had filled his bag with goodies, I asked for some money. He said, "Do you take a credit card?"

So, why should there be surprise when a child copies less desirable behaviour? For example, on one particular childrearing and parenting TV programme, a toddler was running around the house, swearing at her parents. The father was trying to do his best, but shouting: "How many times have I told you, will you *effing* stop using that word!" How many parents do you hear shouting, "Will you stop shouting at me!"? No wonder children receive mixed messages. And yes, of course, I was the perfect mother at all times!

At a very early stage of development, a child will begin to understand that some things they do are 'right and good', and some are 'wrong and bad'. In addition, they will associate certain words and actions with these 'right/good' or 'wrong/bad' behaviours. If a 'wrong/bad' behaviour is given attention, then it is hardly surprising that the child may repeat it, if it is attention that they want and need. They may be learning early on to accept the pain in order to get the pleasure.

Defining ourselves

Illustration

I knew two attractive, smart women who developed rheumatoid arthritis (RA) in their twenties. They were both married with children. Linda almost immediately became an invalid and blamed every negative thing in her life on RA. She had a handsome husband who cared for her, moved to a beautiful house and had no financial worries. Her life revolved around the RA, so conversation became limited. She *became* RA.

The other woman is a schoolfriend, Ailsa Bosworth. Her life over the following 35 years has been full of numerous operations, increasing pain and disability, business challenges and family tragedy. Throughout that time I have never known Ailsa without a smile, even through the tears. She is full of hope and always talking about the next project. Eleven years ago, frustrated by the lack of specialised support for RA suffers, she hassled doctors, politicians and pharmaceutical companies, and founded the National Rheumatoid Arthritis Society (www.nras.org.uk), of which she is still chief executive ten years later. She works long days in two jobs, has a great social life and a home and husband. She *is not* RA, she *has* RA.

I also know of people with chronic conditions who are talented and capable, but who have become dependent on others. They may have most of their needs met, but not healthily. They introduce themselves as their problem: "I'm a depressive", "I'm an alcoholic", "I'm phobic", "I'm a victim". That is not who they *are*, it is what they *have*. They are not their problem – they are so much more. For example, the London 2012 Paralympics showed us that people can achieve extraordinary things with disabilities that are more challenging, while many people sit at home doing very little. One group is living, the others are just existing.

Personal experience

I was a 'naughty girl'. It says so in my school report, and I was continually told off: I don't think there was a classroom that I did not stand outside from the age of 4 to 16. Detentions served no useful purpose at all – they certainly weren't a deterrent. My mother's wrath might have been, but I learned to forge her signature. I learned to lie well, too.

I certainly knew right from wrong, but sometimes didn't really understand why something was wrong. As I grew up, I developed a 'So what?' attitude, as I couldn't seem to do much right at times. I grew up with a sense of injustice at what didn't seem fair: that turned into a double-edged sword. Many of my adult activities have been motivated in a helpful way by that sense of injustice, but the mini-me aged about ten, saying "it's not fair", has hijacked me on too many occasions to be useful. She will still attempt to get me to listen to her at times, although I am feeling more grown up these days and tell her to "Shut up and go away!"

So when did things change for me, and how? Little by little, and only when I could see the possible results of my actions and take personal responsibility for them. Moments of clarity occur, when suddenly the possible consequences reveal themselves in all their glory. Unfortunately, it does not happen all at once on one day, when we are 14 – I only wish it did. Emotional maturity is not much different from physical maturity in that respect.

One day, when I was ten years old and on my own in a shop, I took some sweets from a shop counter and slipped them into my coat pocket. I knew I was stealing. I had got into severe trouble a few months before for doing something similar when my mother was in a grocer's shop with me. I have no idea why I continued with the behaviour, when I knew it could only lead to trouble. Knowing a little about the brain, I can only think that it was impulsive behaviour, when the short-term gain obliterated any vision of long-term pain of getting into trouble.

One of my mother's favourite sayings came out when I had got into some sort of trouble. I would say, "I didn't think" and she would come back at me before I had even finished the sentence: "That's right – you just don't think." Now I am older, I know why I didn't think. My brain was developing, and it had not reached the point where I could understand and visualise the consequences of my actions. This is where I have a problem with people who insist that children who get into trouble obviously have not been taught right from wrong. I certainly knew right from wrong, but did not fully understand the consequences of any 'wrong' action. Punishment did not really help; it seemed to confirm negative feelings.

Immature brains are unable to process the difference between the short-term and the long-term in their thinking. Children's behaviour and emotionally immature adults tend towards being impulsive, where short-term gain is paramount and little thought is given to the long-term results. I carried on stealing and shoplifting until I was 18. I never stole clothes or big items, I wasn't brave enough for that, but magazines and sweets mostly. One infamous Christmas I remember acquiring small stocking filler presents for all the family from a local department store – I am not proud of this, but it is a fact, and acts as a teaching tale.

What happened to make me stop? Why then and there? I was at college and in the local newsagents. The assistant moved away and my hand went out in its usual fashion to take a chocolate bar. The assistant moved back more quickly than I expected, so I stopped. In that moment, I saw my future ahead of me – one of being found out, being thrown out of college, losing my friends and future career. I never shoplifted again.

As I have learned about the brain, I believe that my brain hemispheres switched in those few seconds, and I went from thinking with my emotional, irrational brain to my logical, rational brain. We shall never really know. I am just extremely grateful that it did.

Dealing with temptation

I can resist anything but temptation.

Oscar Wilde

Some unhelpful behaviours, such as drug taking, I never even started. Despite being a rebellious teenager, the first time I was offered drugs, I remember seeing an uncertain future and declined. The tragedy is that my wonderfully talented friend, Petra, who I was with, moved on to heroin. She gave that up, but not the alcohol, and eventually died a premature death in her sixties – not before bringing up two beautiful children though, and very strictly too. She did not want the same to befall her children in times when drugs are commonplace.

Personal experience

As a teenager, I was taken to see some sort of child guidance people, but was not prescribed 'unsuitable' medication. It didn't happen in those days. Bad kids were locked away in borstals, which I was threatened with many times – not that threats did any good, they generally don't with children if they are unrealistic and not carried out.

I did manage to just stay this side of the law and often have to remind myself, when becoming a little too judgemental, that "There but for the grace of God, go I." I met an old headmistress in my late twenties and told her that I'd turned out all right in the end. Her reply? "I knew you would, you had spirit." A little pastoral care might not have gone amiss at the time, but that did not feature at the school until two decades later.

To those people who may think that I was not taught right from wrong, I most certainly was – but it was not until I was able to see and understand the consequences of my actions that I started to change my behaviour. I could not do that until my emotional brain matured, around the age of 18.

Reflection

On a workshop tour of Australia, my husband and I were staying in a bed and breakfast in Sydney: Sandra ran the business from her family home. One night there was a great deal of door slamming and shouting; I didn't like to say anything, but left one of my work books by the bedside when I left that morning. When I got back, Sandra asked if she could have a word, having seen the book as she tidied my room.

Sandra told me that her older daughter had experienced a nasty incident, and was blaming her for bringing them to Australia from the UK ten years previously. Sandra was feeling extremely guilty. We spoke at length, and discussed where her daughter could get support. The next day, Sandra told me that what had helped her own guilt was when I said that had she stayed in the UK, it is more than likely that a negative life event would have occurred at some point in her daughter's life anyway. Her daughter may then have turned round and said that it was Sandra's fault for not going to Australia when they had the opportunity.

Do you have tendency to blame? What or who do you blame? There was a time in my life that I wanted to blame others for my misfortunes; however, I knew that if I carried on it was not going to help my future, and friends would become fed up talking to me. Then I chose a role model. Not 'a positive role model', because often there can be something unreachable about them.

Instead, I chose a 'negative role model': a woman, down-at-the-mouth with long, lanky blonde hair, who used to come into the shop I worked in. She always mentioned at the checkout how her husband had left her and her son: a small, sad-looking boy. Nine years later she was doing exactly the same, except her hair seemed lankier, her mouth more turned down, and her teenage son even more miserable. Every time I found myself about to go into a blaming rant, I thought of this woman. I never wanted to be like that, so I stopped. Twenty years later she still pops into my life sometimes, when I need her.

Do you need a 'negative role model' to deter you from blaming someone or something? Who would you choose?

Chapter 13

'Why should I? What's the point?': meaning and purpose

I went to a bookstore and asked the saleswoman, "Where's the self-help section?" She said if she told me, it would defeat the purpose.

George Carlin

Many of the examples given in this book could come under several chapters, because they illustrate emotional needs from several angles. The following story illustrates the importance of having a meaning and purpose to each day, but it can show just as well the value of friendship, community and being valued.

Every weekday, an elderly woman caught a bus from her home and went into her local town. There, she went to the cafe in a department store for a coffee. Over time the assistants got to know her and her circumstances. One morning she did not turn up: the assistants guessed that something may be wrong and got permission to go to her home, where they found her collapsed on the floor. Calling an ambulance, they possibly saved her life.

It's so easy not to bother, isn't it? To just do the minimum and not make an effort. That is fine once in a while, and fine if you are not experiencing any unhappiness and frustration with your life. However, what about when life does not feel fine? Have circumstances changed, for example, relocation, retirement, ill-health, redundancy, divorce, children leaving home? Have attitudes and behaviour changed accordingly? If not, why not? So often, along with "Why should I?" comes "What's the point?". The point is that you are not happy, and something needs to change. Sometimes we need to search for new meaning, and sometimes events present themselves with opportunities.

There is debate among linguists as to whether the word for 'crisis' in the Chinese language is an amalgam of 'danger' and 'opportunity'. Whether this is true or not, it gives food for thought.

In 2001 there was an outbreak of foot-and-mouth disease among cattle in the UK. It caused devastation for farmers, who had to watch as their livestock was piled high on burning pyres. Ten years later, the farmers who survived well were those who, once over the shock of losing their livelihood, had looked at other opportunities that their land and buildings could offer.

In February 2003, there was a national protest about the Iraq War. The focus was on a march in London. The television news showed various people and groups getting ready to take part; one film showed a group painting slogans on a sheet. An older woman talked about her feelings about the war and the march: she added that since she had got involved with the local anti-war group, her depression had gone.

In each of the categories mentioned above, there will be people who experience depression, anxiety and non-specific physical symptoms when faced with these major life changes. There also will be many other people who experience similar events and who not only survive the changes, but thrive too. This may be a challenging statement for some people:

It is not events that cause depression, it is how we react to them.

Or as my friend and colleague, Sue Hanisch, says:

Depression is nature's way of saying that you should change something about your life.

Some may be unhappy with that view, but I have never met anyone who has recovered from a period of depression – including severe depression – who has not changed something that they are doing in their lives. It could be making changes at home, in the workplace or socially. It could be with diet, exercise, relaxation or just attitude. Any change bringing about a helpful reaction will change brain chemistry, and without the need for medication – although of course, this can take initial effort.

The importance of choice

There is no doubt that life events can be deeply upsetting, disturbing and challenging, but we can make choices, and it is important to remember this.

In everyday life, we watch TV and something comes on that we do not want to watch. We press a button on a remote control and bingo! – we are faced with something different. We do the same with radio programmes and music players: instant change with no effort. Often, we cannot even be bothered to press a button, and just put up with something we don't really want to listen to or watch. It is our choice and it has made us lazy.

The meaning and purpose of our lives is not something that we really give thought to as young children: we just get on and do what we are told to do: going to school, visiting friends and relatives, following a sport, attending religious meetings. At a very young age we may challenge a suggestion, but when we ask "Why should I?", the response is "Because I say so." End of discussion – our life choices are made by someone else.

As we mature, we learn to make decisions for ourselves by giving ourselves the reasons why it may be a good idea or not to do something. Our circumstances change and we need to change along with them, taking responsibility for those changes. So if you find yourself or someone else saying, "Why should I?", you can give yourself some very good reasons. The problem is that many people do not want to make the effort involved: often, it is because they want someone to do it for them. The more we 'baby' our children, the greater the problem becomes.

Retirement, redundancy, 'empty nest' syndrome and other life events can leave us looking for new purpose and meaning to our lives. They can be combined with feelings of loss (see Chapter 10). I have met many people who, through life events, are left needing to find new purpose and meaning: some appear to want to be spoon-fed with new experiences, and wonder why they become down when a new life does not suddenly appear on their doorstep.

I have often wondered what happens to sports stars who reach the height of their fame and fortune at a very young age – often before they are emotionally mature. I cannot think that it is easy to build up to the heights, hit them and then come down the other side before you are 30. It is the same with child film stars. The TV sports presenter and former England international, Gary Lineker, was talking about his career as one of England's top footballers and his friend Paul Gascoigne:

> When you're a footballer you're treated like a child. You will have breakfast at this time. You will eat this or that. You will get on the bus at 10am. You will have people shouting at you. You will go to bed the night before a game at a reasonable hour. Whereas in TV we can have a few drinks the night before. We can

have dinner. I don't have people shouting at me, I'm more in control. I feel more of a grown-up. But I'm lucky because I've found something else to do. Whereas Gazza hasn't. (*Daily Mail*, 8 March 2013)

Footballers have time on their hands and the mind can make mischief, if bored. A footballer once told me that the weekday afternoons on non-playing days are the worst: practice has finished and the time is their own. Playing golf seems a good way of occupying non-playing hours, but gambling often fills the gap, especially on the horses, which race in the afternoon. Another footballer told me that gambling not only filled the time, but gave him a buzz. The buzz reminded him of being a little boy at his mother's elbow as she played the fruit machines in an arcade.

Resisting change

Another life event is when children move away from home: 'empty nest syndrome', as mentioned previously. This is an excellent reason to find new meaning and purpose, although there are parents – often mothers – who are not prepared to let their children go.

'Failed fledglings' is a term that I read in a newspaper in May 2013. The article was about the number of children who are returning home in their twenties. In the same week I read the following extract in an article about the singer, Maureen Nolan.

It is a very different picture back at Maureen's home in Blackpool, where she lives with husband Ritchie Hoyle, 48, a music tour manager. Their son Danny, 24, has just moved back in with his fianceé Maddison, 23, and daughter Sienna, two.

"It's a mad house. Danny was floundering a bit with bills so I said he was welcome to come and live with us. I'm thrilled.

"My husband is still a bit traumatised, with the baby jumping on him every morning – but I grew up in a mad household so I love it. I didn't ever want him to leave," says Maureen. (*Daily Mail*, 11 May 2013)

Will this really benefit the adult son and his family?

If parents will not let go of their children, often they grow up with emotional health problems. Nature did not intend children to hang around the home, but to venture out and find a mate. The way that small, scrunched-up, fledging birds are encouraged out of their nest and have no option but to fly, although they have never done it before, is a miracle of nature.

Personal experience

When I first found myself living on my own, my children having left to go to university, they were wonderfully supportive, with lots of comforting hugs that I craved. It would have been so easy to keep them close rather than let them go. I remember my daughter, Louise, home for the weekend, saying one Saturday night "Is it okay if we go out tonight?" "Of course, off you go," I replied cheerfully. It was the last thing I wanted.

Illustration

Maureen married Tony, and set up home with his mother. Tony had assured her that his mother was not well and would die soon. Tony's mother lasted longer than the marriage.

A salutary fable

This is one of the teaching tales I have used. It is helpful for people who tend towards being overprotective towards their children. A king and queen had a child whom they loved dearly. They didn't want him to come to any harm. They protected him and would not let him go outside the castle walls, fearing that he would be killed by the wild animals outside. They made sure that everything he needed was provided for him in the castle.

The king and queen ordered a room to be painted with glorious creatures, replicating the animals outside the castle. So the painters worked on a magnificent mural on the high walls, depicting the animal kingdom. One day, the boy was wandering through the castle and passed the room being painted. The door was open, but nobody was there. He marvelled at what he saw, and wanted to get nearer the animals, so he climbed one of the ladders, reached out at the top to touch an animal – and fell off and was killed.

Managing change and finding new meaning

Finding a meaning and purpose to our lives alters as life events bring changes for us to deal with: some good, others not so.

We have plans. We have expectations. Then we find ourselves up in the air, our lives tumbling around us in a kaleidoscope of confusion. Life settles again, but things are different: they are not how we thought they would be. However, as I have pointed out to clients when they have told me, "Things will never change" – does any week turn out exactly how you thought it would? It helps put things into perspective.

Personal experience

In 1994, I remarried and moved to a city 250 miles away from familiar surroundings. I chose to give up my career in retailing and a busy social life, and take a leap of faith: faith in my new husband, Alex. There is no doubt that it was a risk, but by then I knew that

I was resourceful and adaptable, so felt that I could cope with the massive change. Everything that had been my meaning and purpose in life had changed. My children were adults and pursuing lives away from their hometown. The secure job that I thought I would have until retirement was no more. I had even changed my name.

I gave myself two weeks to get unpacked and sorted out in the flat. There was no Facebook or Twitter, and emails were in their infancy. The one thing I knew for certain was that no one was going to come to the door, ring the bell and say to me, "Alison, we have been waiting for you. Welcome." I didn't know the city, the surrounding countryside or anyone living anywhere nearby.

My first priority? To find a cafe that I could take visitors to when they came. How quickly times change: nowadays we can walk into any large town or city and find any number of coffee shops. In 1994, there were lots of cafes, but no coffee shop chains. I took a newspaper with me and visited different cafes. Number one task achieved.

Now, to find something to do. I wondered whether I could find some reception work – as long as it involved interacting with people, I didn't mind, but I wasn't so sure about retailing. My previous job had spoilt me for other workplaces. I looked in the Yellow Pages and found an agency, but it was for nannies and nurses. I had not thought about resurrecting my old work experience, so nevertheless popped into their office and asked if they wanted a part-time nursery nurse who hadn't worked in that line for ten years. They jumped at the chance. Most people on their books wanted full-time positions, and there was a need for emergency cover in some cases. One of those cases was later to change my life in ways I could never have imagined. Number two task achieved.

Alex's colleagues were friendly and welcoming, but I needed something of my own. Next stop, the library – there would be lots of information there. There was, and I visited a few groups before I settled on something I was interested in. Number three task achieved. Next was to feel involved in the community. After visiting churches of every type, we decided on one. Number four task achieved.

It took a little time, but I settled into my new home, a new job and a new hobby. As a result I made new friends, but I had to do it – no one did it for me.

Managing sudden or unexpected change

Katie's husband, James, died. He had been deteriorating steadily, and had needed more care from Katie. Slowly, over a period of months, Katie's social life had dwindled and was replaced by activities specifically for James. Her availability for voluntary work reduced until she knew that she could not do any at all.

James's death came more quickly than expected and was a bit of a shock in the end, but also a blessing in the circumstances. Despite the shock, Katie still had to manage the funeral arrangements. She knew she had to keep busy. To begin with, there is always so much to do, and then comes the solitude. She said: "Every time I miss James, I realise that I don't miss the illness at all."

Family elsewhere in the country kept her occupied, as did administration matters. Her mind drifted towards what she should do next in her life. She told me, "James was my daily purpose; now he's gone. I must find another purpose." Work was an option, but she was past retirement age, so knew that it was likely to be in the voluntary sector. There were plenty of alternatives for this highly capable woman, but she felt restless and, while justifying all her options, felt that they were not quite right for her. Then one day, she was walking down the street and experienced a 'Eureka!' moment: "I want to travel!"

Katie and James had made great plans for retirement, including travelling. Initially there was sadness that these plans had ceased. Or had they? Katie thought about it. She could still travel. She had some means. She had the time. She had the freedom. She could still make plans, but they were different from the original ones. Katie had new meaning and purpose to her life. Her future was in her hands.

She didn't feel that she ought do it – she just wanted to do it. In fact, she needed to do it.

Barriers to change

So often we put up our own barriers to stop doing something. Maybe something that is out of our comfort zone.

We say to ourselves: "Why should I?"

The answer is: "Why shouldn't you?"

There is also another common answer that adults give to children: "Because I say so." That is necessary on occasions, but as adults there should be times when we question quite *who* is telling us what to do, *what* they are telling us to do and *why* they need to tell us. Is it for their good rather than ours?

Reflection

This exercise can be used personally or for members of the family. Take some blank paper, or open a blank document on your computer screen. Think about something you would like to change in your life or someting you want to achieve that seems out of reach. Use the sheet to have a look at your goals and the steps that you need to take to achieve them. Identify and note down the three types of goal:

1. Short-term goals – today, tomorrow, next week.

2. Medium-term goals – the next few months.

3. Long-term goals – next year, five years' time, ten years' time.

The SMARTER nmemonic is a useful technique to examine your goals. Take a look through what you have written down, and think about each goal under these headings.

S – Specific

M – Measured

A – Attainable

R – Realistic

T – Timed

E – Evaluate

R – Reassess

Chunking

Another good technique is 'chunking', which is based on our natural circadian rhythms. The human brain switches brain hemispheres every 90 minutes. Have you ever wondered why taking a break when stuck on a piece of work can make a difference, and a problem can be solved? The brain has taken a natural break. If you have trouble organising yourself in the day, think of a school timetable. Chunk up the day into periods of an hour to 90 minutes – use your brain's natural rhythms. This can make a big difference to your personal productivity.

Task and treat

If a task isn't rewarding but has to be done, give yourself a treat to look forward to after the task is completed. I save reading a newspaper or magazine as my treat. It is much easier to make a donkey move forwards by putting a carrot in front of it than pushing from behind.

Chapter 14

'They've got more than me': personal value and self-esteem

No one can make you feel inferior without your consent.
Eleanor Roosevelt

In summer 2012 I was part of a glorious social experiment (not that it felt like that, but I do hope academics were studying the phenomenon). I was part of a volunteer workforce of more than 70,000 people, where everyone had equal status: the highly acclaimed 'Games Makers' at the London 2012 Olympics. We came from all parts of the UK and further afield, all shapes, sizes, ages, genders, ethnicities and religions. From the cap on our heads to the trainers on our feet, we wore the same clothes – as did the paid managers. If the women's trousers were a better fit for the men, they wore them, and vice-versa. We all mucked in with whatever work was required. There were team leaders, and I noticed in some teams that they wore armbands, but not in ours.

There were meal breaks and quiet times. During those times we got to find out a little about our colleagues, and what wonderfully varied backgrounds we all had. To pass the time in one quiet period, a game was played: we all had to write down three facts about ourselves. Two were true, one was false. The pieces of paper were read out, and people guessed which one was false. I always enjoy this game because people assume so much by a voice or a look – and can get it so wrong.

> **Example**
>
> Justin stood at the front of the church, dressed in his clerical robes. His sermon was on making assumptions and judging people. He started to undo his robe, to the congregation's amusement: underneath he was wearing a football referee's uniform – it was a job he did in his spare time. Justin's point was that he was more than just a vicar, and that the congregation only saw, and possibly judged him on, his appearance in robes.

Usually we make judgements about people from their appearance, their voices and then their environment. Take a look at the following list:

- status
- self-esteem
- self-regard
- personal value
- self-confidence
- self-respect
- ego
- self-assurance
- self-worth

From my perspective they all mean one thing: feeling good enough. It does not matter what someone might name it, but I have yet to meet anyone with an emotional health problem or mental health problem who doesn't feel 'not good enough' in one or more areas of their lives. Which areas? Well, whichever one where they probably felt 'not good enough' to have certain emotional needs met as a child, and still feel a fear of 'not being good enough' to get them met in adult life.

This is different for everyone. One person may have no problem feeling good enough to achieve a job of work, but in personal relationships feel inadequate and experience childish emotions. Another person may be loved and love in return on adult terms, but when asked to deliver a presentation, is swamped by their mini-me, reminding them that they are a failure.

In researching this subject and checking that I was on the right track, I looked, and still look, for evidence in real-life examples. The best of these are found in 'profile' articles in newspapers and magazines. There are many professional sportspeople and performers who win competitions, awards and praise from their peers, but admit that they are disabled by self-doubt and a fear of not being good enough – disabled enough to take their own lives or live a life dependent on medication, alcohol or drugs. I have quoted from some of them in this book.

When I was a little girl I used to enjoy picture puzzle books. There was always a puzzle with some children holding the leads to dogs, but had them all mixed up. The puzzle was to match up the people A, B, C and D with their dogs, 1, 2, 3 and 4. I was reminded of this sort of puzzle when I realised that whatever problem someone came to see me with, I could match it up with a feeling of not being good enough to get an emotional need met when they were younger.

For some years now, I have set a test of credibility. You can try it too. It might be a 'misery memoir' or profile in a magazine where the person writes or talks about a problem that they have had in their life. I scan the paragraphs and always find it: they didn't feel good enough in some area of their life. It is always there.

This is where I have a problem with labels, especially psychiatric labels.

I vowed that there would be no use of the word 'issue' in this book, but it is impossible when wanting to illustrate a point. The word that should be used in the majority of cases is 'problem', but political correctness and positive psychology have hijacked it. 'Problem' is negative, 'issue' is not – up to a point. The word 'issue' is overused: I knew things had had gone too far when someone was talking about their vacuum cleaner having 'issues'. On the TV programme, *Great British Bake Off*, someone had icing issues. I despair.

The previously mentioned DSM-5 is the diagnostic bible for mental health disorders (see Chapter 10). However, in medicalising normal behaviours, it is creating complexity and some weird-sounding diagnoses: for example, 'oppositional defiant disorder' (ODD). I would like to suggest some simpler explanations for a few disorders:

- Abandonment issues – not feeling good enough to be wanted or loved.
- Self-esteem issues – feeling frightened of not being thought good enough.
- Personality disorder – not feeling good enough, and childish in a number of areas of life.
- Attachment issues – feeling insecure as an adult, hanging on to childhood.

There will be others too.

There are also behaviours that, it has been suggested, are connected with having too high self-esteem: gang leaders and bullies are among the people demonstrating this. I would suggest that somewhere in the psychological make-up of these adults is a mini-me screaming in distress. Bullies rule by fear, but somewhere in the bully's make-up there is a frightened child driving their ego.

When I had a practice, I had a large picture in the reception area. It contained the following words that I had found on a postcard. I used to think that if the adults who came into the practice had experienced some of the following wisdom, they probably would not be needing help.

If children live with criticism, they learn to condemn.

If children live with hostility, they learn to fight.

If children live with fear, they learn to be apprehensive.

If children live with pity, they learn to feel sorry for themselves.

If children live with ridicule, they learn to feel shy.

If children live with jealousy, they learn to feel envy.

If children live with shame, they learn to feel guilty.

If children live with encouragement, they learn confidence.

If children live with tolerance, they learn patience.

If children live with praise, they learn appreciation.

If children live with acceptance, they learn to love.

If children live with approval, they learn to like themselves.

If children live with recognition, they learn it is good to have a goal.

If children live with sharing, they learn generosity.

If children live with honesty, they learn truthfulness.

If children live with fairness, they learn justice.

If children live with kindness and consideration, they learn respect.

If children live with security, they learn to have faith in themselves and in those about them.

If children live with friendliness, they learn the world is a nice place in which to live.

Dorothy Law Nolte

I also added at the bottom: "Time is money, but the best thing you can spend on your children is time." I wish I had had these words when I ran the toddler group – I feel they should be given out to every parent.

Self-esteem and materialism

Another challenging area can be achieving a level of self-esteem through work or a leisure activity. If that position is removed for any reason, such as retirement, a change of domestic circumstances, financial problems and so on, adapting can be tough if all your eggs are in one basket.

> **Example**
>
> Freddy had climbed the career ladder to a reasonable position, one where he was meeting people who were thought important in his work. Some were famous. I asked him: "Do you feel important now?" "No", came his reply, "It could all end tomorrow." He had seen people who had been front page news become yesterday's news and feel lost.

This is why we have status symbols. Some insecure people will feel more secure with material items that advertise their achievements, rather than relying on their own selves.

As a 'Games Maker', one of my volunteer colleagues worked as a teacher at a public school. We were talking about the toll that the recent financial collapse and recession had caused. He said that many parents had been hit hard, but the school had done its best to keep the pupils without disrupting exams, although this had had a knock-on effect on the school's finances. He mentioned that the children coped with the reduced circumstances better than the parents. I could believe that.

In her book *Guard a Silver Sixpence*, Felicity Davis relates that she grew up, left her abusive home and became a teacher against the odds. She writes:

> I wish I could say that from then on it was all 'Educating Rita' and happily ever after, but real life isn't like that.

> I was now earning the kind of wage I thought only other people earned, and for a while I tried to be someone else. I made the huge mistake of moving us out of the comfortable terraced ex-council home on the estate where my boys had put down their roots, and into a five-bedroom Victorian villa in the centre of old Scarborough which I bought with a huge mortgage.

> At about the same time – because problems never arrive on their own – I was forced to admit that I couldn't really afford the swanky Victorian villa. I could just about pay the mortgage, but I hadn't taken into account the most basic expenses, such as the heating bill for such a big house, or the endless maintenance costs. We'd been there for two and a half years while I pretended it was working, and I was overstretched and on the verge of bankruptcy. The house had also robbed us of something more important than solvency. What I had thought would be a wonderful family home had instead become

a house-share. The boys were old enough to be independent – they were 19, 20 and 26 – but even when they weren't on the other side of Scarborough spending time with their friends back on the estate, they were shut up in separate, distant parts of the house. Communication between us had all but broken down.

Personal experience

Many people regard shop assistants as pretty low in social standing. I worked with people who were shop assistants for a variety of reasons, and some were highly qualified in other fields. I have challenged parents who dismiss a child with: "He/she will end up as a shop assistant or hairdresser." Shock tactics can work sometimes, and informing people of my own retail experience can lead to an adjustment of their preconceptions.

When I was still in retailing, I was invited to Sunday lunch with friends of a friend. The host was a professor, Bernard. This was the sort of company I never mixed with, and I thought that my lack of academic qualifications would be obvious. My friend and I arrived, were offered a drink, and embarked on some small talk. "And what do you do?", the professor's wife, Angela, asked. Inwardly, I took a deep breath and thought, "Go for it!" "I'm a supermarket checkout manager," I replied. Her response stunned me: "Oh, how brave of you to admit it." The invisible walls of imagined superiority collapsed in front of my eyes. I realised that I wasn't the most ignorant person in the room.

I started to move in more academic circles and there were more dinners, some quite formal. At one dinner, after the meal, the host, Bernard, decided to ask everyone's opinion on some matter – a matter of which I knew nothing. Fortunately, as he went round the table, I was about sixth in line, so had time to think. What I didn't expect, was that when he reached me, he said, "Oh Alison, you won't be able to say anything," and prepared to move on. I felt insulted.

So I said that I did have something to say. I cannot remember what, but I was able to contribute some 'bon mot' combining the subject matter and some chocolate-tasting work I was doing, a job I still have. Chocolate is a great social leveller.

Julian was doing well in the legal profession. He had risen up the career ladder and was earning a good salary. The problem was that he was spending more than he was earning and getting into debt problems. Julian's colleagues in the practice had been qualified for some time. They earned high salaries, and had lifestyles to match. Julian admitted that in order to keep up with the office chat, he felt that he had to frequent the same restaurants, hotels and sporting events – then he could hold his own in the conversation.

There was an infamous incident in 1995 when 'rogue trading' by Nick Leeson brought down Barings Bank. Leeson wrote in his book, *Back from the Brink: Coping with Stress*, that it was 'status' or 'self-regard' that had led to the disaster. He asked someone else to do a job that he was meant to be doing and they made a mistake, so rather than admit that this was what had happened, he tried to cover it up – but the problem grew until the bank collapsed.

Mistakes are made all the time – that is normal. Some will be due to lack of the right tools for the jobs, whether intellectual and otherwise – but some will be because people cannot admit to their mistakes.

Reflection

In childhood we acquire labels. These labels are given to us by other people.

Examine the labels you apply to yourself. Every single label is a boundary or a limit of one kind or another.

Wayne Dyer

Wayne Dyer is correct.

When one of the founders of the Apple organisation, Steve Jobs, died, the airwaves and internet were full of tributes and some of his quotes. These are my favourites.

"Your time is limited, so don't waste it living someone else's life. Don't be trapped by dogma – which is living with the results of other people's thinking."

"Don't let the noise of others' opinions drown out your own inner voice – and most important, have the courage to follow your heart and intuition. They somehow already know what you truly want to become. Everything else is secondary."

Putting the two quotes together, I have come up with: "Don't go round wearing a label that someone else has attached to you. If you believe it, it could wear you down."

Here are some examples of negative labels.

"You're our anxious one."
"You're still our baby."
"You're stupid/a waste of space/were never wanted/hopeless."
"You'll never achieve anything."

"You're just like your mother/father."
"You're slow to learn, sure to fail."
"You'll end up in the gutter."

It is not only negative labels that can cause problems; filling someone with overly positive expectations may not be helpful either. There are many people who leave school believing that they are 'clever' and 'special', who then find the world full of other 'clever' and 'special' people. In the summer of 2013, the exam results again showed that top grades meant that the pupil had worked hard and done well, but so had hundreds of others and a university place was not guaranteed.

Exercise

1. Think of a belief that you have about yourself.

2. Think of it being written on a label that you wear every day.

3. Who gave you that label?

4. When did they give you that label?

5. Why did they give you that label?

6. Have you grown older since you were given that label?

7. Is there any evidence that the label is now out of date, if it was even true in the first place?

8. Remove the label and destroy it.

Chapter 15

'I'm bored': use and misuse of the imagination

Your true traveller finds boredom rather agreeable than painful. It is the symbol of his liberty – his excessive freedom. He accepts his boredom, when it comes, not merely philosophically, but almost with pleasure.

Aldous Huxley

To those readers over a certain age, in childhood was there really ever a day in the year more dull than Good Friday? Certainly, Sundays had their rituals that kept them a quieter day than the rest of the week, but Good Friday was dull, dull, dull. You couldn't say that nowadays, as it becomes another busy shopping day before the Easter break. There is no time for reflection, anyway. Reflection on what – on life? The past, present or future? If any younger reader is in doubt what a Sunday could feel like, then do no more than listen to an episode of Tony Hancock's classic radio comedy, *Hancock's Half Hour*: 'Sunday Afternoon at Home'.

Boredom can provide a time for mischief or good, or just nothing in particular. Whatever it does, it can provide time to use the imagination.

In therapy, the therapist will not see many people with an optimistic nature. In fact, therapists are taught to protect themselves from the negativity that can pour out of a client – sometimes you can feel your own energy start to drain away. Therapists may hear a great deal of fantasy or imagined scenarios in situations involving emotional health problems. I have found that generally, the greater the misuse of the imagination, the more creative talents the client possesses. The more creative talents the client possesses, the easier it is to find resources that they can use for problem-solving. Many people experiencing depression and anxiety disorders show great creativity. This is hardly surprising, as these conditions often involve the misuse of the imagination.

Sometimes I knew what the client's creative skills were, but most of the time it was enjoyable finding out: gardening, woodcraft, cooking, writing, music, painting, languages and so on. I certainly had to stretch my imagination. Only one person out of the hundreds of people I saw was adamant that they were not creative in any way. I had to believe them, but even then I suggested that they may not have discovered their particular skill yet.

I would be working with a completely blank sheet, and gradually the picture of a client's abilities and skills would be revealed – not that they always saw themselves as having skills and abilities. Too often, a person presenting with symptoms of an emotional health disorder would think that there was very little that was positive about them at all.

Are problems real or imagined?

We use our imagination all the time, although I have met people who say that they have no imagination. In practice I became used to people presenting with a bucketload of problems – most of them imagined – who would then tell me that they had no imagination. We all think we know what someone has said, or what they were thinking, and in therapy it is important to find out the facts. In my head I could hear Mr Gradgrind from Charles Dickens' *Hard Times*: "Facts, facts, facts!" The damage that a too-vivid imagination can do is enormous.

> **Example**
>
> In therapy, it is common for a therapist to hear generalisations such as "I've never been any good", "I haven't got any friends" or "I'm hopeless". A client may say that something is their fault or tell you what somebody else thinks of them, but is fuzzy about the exact details. There can also be a tendency towards catastrophising information: "I'm always like this", "It will never change", "It's ruined my life forever". The more information you gather, the more the basic facts can get lost. It is only when the therapist can extract a few facts about a situation that some unhelpful thought processes can be challenged and changed.

Black and white thinking

There is a difference between needing to know the facts around a problem, and 'black and white thinking' which can prevent useful problem-solving. In black and white thinking the client only sees matters in two ways, whereas there are many shades in-between. As a therapist I have particularly enjoyed working with artists and musicians, where it was very easy to help them understand that life was neither coloured black and white, nor made up of only black and white music notes. Sometimes clients with mathematical or scientific brains have been a little more difficult to convince that there is no right or wrong answer.

Using the imagination positively

People experiencing symptoms of depression and anxiety conditions generally exercise an unhealthy misuse of the imagination. As mentioned previously, a healthy use of the imagination is necessary in creative activities.

Illustration

Yasmin was getting quite cross. "I have no imagination," she repeated. From the little information she had told me on that first appointment, it was obvious that indeed she did have an imagination, and an active one too. There were a great many imagined scenarios and few facts. As we talked about her skills and abilities, she agreed with me that she had to have an imagination to do what she did in her life. It also became clear why she thought that she didn't have an imagination.

As a nine-year-old, Yasmin was writing a story in class one day. The teacher rubbished her efforts and told her in a loud voice, in front of the class, that the story was not good enough and that she lacked imagination. Thirty years later, that teacher's view of Yasmin's work ruled her head. The number of people who hang on to something a teacher once said is large. It may have felt traumatic at the time, and still feel like a threat to personal integrity.

Mind over matter

Our imagination can be a useful tool in helping or harming our bodies. For example, at a workshop I attended, the participants had to take their own temperature and write it down. We worked in pairs: each person had to help the other imagine a scenario where they were very cold. Then we took our temperatures again. All of them had gone down – some more significantly than others. The same exercise can be done with taking another person's pulse. Another common exercise in workshops is for the workshop leader to take the group through visualising tasting a lemon: most people will salivate. I salivate just writing this down.

Personal experience

I attended a lecture on the imagination, and the tutor gave the following illustration on one of the most frightening jobs that anyone could be asked to do: public speaking. He asked us to imagine a worst-case scenario along these lines:

1. We arrive on stage, drop our notes, fall over trying to pick them up, break our arm, get taken to hospital, pick up a hospital bug, and die.

Then he asked us to imagine the best case scenario:

2. We arrive on stage and deliver an outstanding presentation. People give us a standing ovation. In the audience is a Hollywood producer – he whisks us to Los Angeles, where we become a major TV star and find fame and fortune.

By the time he finished these two scenarios, the audience was laughing at the silliness of it all. His comment was that while both scenarios could possibly happen, the likelihood would be somewhere in the middle. The presentation will not be the best that everyone has heard, but it will not be the worst either. Then he went on to talk about how the imagination can be used healthily too: we can imagine ourselves doing the task, and improve our chances of succeeding.

Imagining the worst

If you hear anyone say, when a disaster has befallen them, "I knew that would happen", you know that they have probably been imagining the worst. We can jump to conclusions too quickly and make mistakes. For example, I lived in a flat with the garage at the bottom of the garden. Someone had parked in the way and I couldn't park in the garage. Then I saw my chance: I nipped downstairs and out of the back door, leaving the front door open, got in the car and parked it in the garage.

I returned to the flat to find my flatmate, Catherine, had arrived home through the front entrance and was highly agitated. "We've had a burglar!" she exclaimed.

She had come home, found the front door open and no one in. She looked out of the window to see me driving into the garage: obviously, I was arriving home myself. No – her brain had taken in various pieces of information and gone "Snap", except the picture was wrong. Catherine did have a tendency towards feeling anxious and to think the worst.

Personal experience

When I was 11 years old, I was attending a weekly hospital clinic for a problem I had with my feet. As previously mentioned, I was also in trouble for stealing.

My father took me to the hospital for my regular appointment. I was surprised to be taken into a different room. There was a man and a woman. The woman took me into another room, while the man talked to my father. I was encouraged to draw and do colouring while I readily chatted to the woman. I asked who did all the brightly coloured pictures on the walls. She replied that some children had difficulty talking and were able to draw instead. Being unable to talk has never been one of my problems.

She asked me about why I was stealing. I remember distinctly asking her not to tell anyone what I was about to tell her. Not that I can remember what I said.

As my father and I left, I turned around to wave. The woman was talking to the man. All these years later, I now realise that she could have been saying anything, but to my eyes and in my imagination, she was telling him what I had said. That, of course, would have happened later, and I would not have seen it. I believe that my intense feelings of mistrust in figures of authority arose from that day. In many ways, it has served me well, but it has caused me a whole lot of problems too.

The confused imagination

In playing 'snap' with memory-matches, the English language can cause a few problems of incorrect pattern-matching.

Illustration

Sally was living with her son, Ben. I popped in for a cup of coffee and a chat. The atmosphere was not good, there was a distinct chill between them. The young man had experienced a couple of years of mental health problems, but was getting better. After some difficult times, Ben had found an outdoor activity that he loved: being part of a local volunteer conservation group. On this particular day, the group had been involved in some heavy work on the local moors. He arrived home after a hard day's work, and saw his mother in the garden picking apples from the tree.

"Hi Ben," said Sally, "I'm stuck up this tree."

"Hi mum," said Ben, "I'm going to have a bath and go on the computer."

As Ben told me later, "I thought she meant that she was 'stuck' up the tree – in the same way that I might have said, "I've been 'stuck' on the moors all day."

Unfortunately, what Sally meant was that she was indeed stuck in the apple tree: she could not get down and was beginning to panic. As a result, Sally had difficulty thinking straight as she had become emotionally aroused. She saw Ben go back in the house. Instead of shouting louder and explaining her predicament, she imagined that Ben had chosen to ignore her in his selfish, teenage way. A neighbour saw her, came round and helped her down. Sally was furious and would not listen to Ben's more than reasonable explanation.

Reflection

I use this reflection regularly when my mind starts to wander in an unhelpful way. It helps neutralise my imaginings, reduce emotional arousal and help manage the given situation.

Take an experience that you are going to have. If you cannot think of anything in the present, then recall one from the recent past: it could be a journey, a health problem or a domestic event.

How is your self-dialogue? What are you saying to yourself?

Are your expectations negative or positive?

What are the facts? Could you be taking a flight of fantasy?

Is this the worst day, weather, food, meeting or journey that you have ever had?

Could you change your self-dialogue to be more realistic? Would that be a helpful way of managing the situation?

These questions can help to deal with life events in the present, when the mind can catastrophise. They can help to put things into perspective. For example:

When life was particularly difficult, Val gave me a gift of a ceramic bowl of cherries. There was a note attached: "This is for the days when life isn't a bowl of cherries." I can look at those cherries and remember how challenging those times were, and realise how far I have come since then.

The quality of your life can be dependent on the quality of your self-dialogue.

Chapter 16

'Ouch! It hurts': pain

> *If you pick it, it won't get better.*
>
> **Anon**

This chapter may ruffle a few feathers and I know some people will fiercely disagree with me. This book is a personal insight, based on personal observations. Other viewpoints are allowed.

Life leaves us with emotional and physical scars. We know better than to pick at the physical ones, so why is it considered helpful to pick at emotional ones?

Treatment for a physical wound is usually to keep it clean, cover it and let it heal naturally. However, if the instruction for healing is to pop along to the doctor's surgery once a week, where a nurse takes the covering off, removes the new skin growth, sticks a scalpel into the wound and prods it, this would be called medical negligence. Yet, somehow the accepted belief for treating emotional wounds is precisely that. Obviously, if someone keeps repeating a damaging behaviour then it is a good idea to find out why that is happening – but it probably does not require so much probing that the wound becomes toxic.

I had been asked to work as a nursery nurse on an acute psychiatric unit, by a nursing agency that employed me. I was supporting a mother with postnatal depression in looking after her baby. After three days, I was asked if I would stay on the unit as a nursing assistant and I ended up staying six years. I worked with hundreds of people covering a wide spectrum of mental health, and certainly emotional health, problems. After a couple of years, I observed a few things that I felt needed further study on my part:

1. The reliance of clients on medication.

2. The revolving door, where clients went out but returned several times.

3. Some clients appeared to become worse than they were before they came in.

I funded my own studies in a diploma in solution-focused, short-term psychotherapy, using cognitive and behavioural therapies. I stayed on the unit until the conflict of interest became too great. I opened a practice, which I ran for ten years. Before the opening, I bought some attractive boxes of tissues for the tables. After all, hadn't the unit been lined with boxes of tissues? Everyone knows that tissues and therapy go together. Then I realised what I was doing: planting the suggestion of crying copiously. It's like saying, "Don't think of a pink elephant". What pops into most people's brains? Exactly – a pink elephant. I removed the boxes of tissues. There wasn't a tissue in sight. I had small, handy packets tucked down the cushion of my seat, but rarely needed to produce them.

A victim mentality

Pain is inevitable. Suffering is optional.
From the Buddhist Noble Eightfold Path

Is it a given that if something awful happens to you, you become a victim? Can you choose to become a victim?

On 23 May 2013 a soldier, Lee Rigby, was the victim of a random and gruesome killing on the streets of London. The media needed to report the incident, but prefer it if people being interviewed are emotional – it makes for better pictures and headlines. This particular incident involved a remarkable woman called Ingrid Loyau-Kennett, who showed an incredible level of calmness in the face of terror and men holding knives, by approaching the assailants and talking to one of them. She was on the radio and in newspapers, retelling her story in a calm and measured way. As the week went by, I became a little concerned as to how she would manage with this constant retelling and picking of the wounds.

A week after the event, Ms Loyau-Kennett was taken back to the place of the incident, which had a carpet of flowers and soft toys. She was interviewed on TV, and I could see her calmness beginning to wobble. In the paper the next day I read that Ms Loyau-Kennett now tries to avoid thinking about the incident. "I don't read anything and try not to watch too much because I don't want to relive these potentially bad memories," she said. She is absolutely right, and I only hope that she is allowed to do that.

The language of victimhood

How is it that two people can experience a similar traumatic event and one person's life seems to be ruined, while the other person recovers? Why does this happen? There can be a mixture of reasons: brain damage, medication side-effects, not having emotional needs met, and secondary gain are among them. For people who choose to become a victim, the language they use can be illuminating.

"X ruined my life" is a commonly used expression. I heard it this year when I attended a college reunion: the college where I studied nursery nursing was also a children's home for the under-fives. There were women in their sixties and a man in his late forties at the reunion. Darren had been a child in the children's home from two weeks to five years, moving on to other homes until adulthood.

How many readers think that it must have been Darren who said it? No, it was one of the alumni attending, Gemma. Recently, she had sold her house in the south and bought a beautiful, large house in her son's partner's hometown in the North, where she didn't know anyone. Her son, partner and grandchild had moved north through redundancy, and it had been a disaster. "I thought we could all live in the house happily ever after." Life is not a fairy story.

We supported and comforted Gemma. She said, "They have ruined my life." Another friend, Louise, whose own daughter has severe problems with addiction, with appalling consequences for the family, said. "No, they have not ruined your life. You are allowing them to ruin your life." There were nods of agreement from others, who knew from their own experiences that she was correct.

Afterwards, a group of us were concerned. The reported behaviour of all the adults left us wondering about the emotional intelligence of them all, and most concerned about the child.

This is not easy to understand or believe. If we look at the difference between those who are victims and those who are not, one of the major differences is those who give control of their lives over to an event or other person, and those who take control of their own life. Those who alter the word 'ruined' to 'changed' agree that 'it changed my life', but they do not allow it to ruin their lives.

I feel I might be hearing a "Yes, but..." from some readers. Have a look around at your friends, family and wider circle. How have people dealt with life experiences? Do events control them, or do they control their responses to events? People who have experienced the grimmest of circumstances have chosen not to become victims, while others have chosen that path.

James, who attended the reunion, sent us an email afterwards:

Dear All

It was delightful to meet up with many of you in the evening. It's hard to explain just how pleased it makes me to be able to meet and talk with people who knew me as child. You made a big difference to my life way back then and it continues to have an impact on me today. Growing up in care can leave some people with a sense of loss or abandonment but I can say that I have never felt like that. In fact I feel blessed to have had so many people looking out for me and to me you are all part of my family. As a child I used to tell people that I was brought up by angels and, to me, that's what you always will be.

Lots of love,

James

It could be so easy for James to be going through life 'out of control', blaming his mother, an unknown father and various institutions. He could be wearing the unhelpful label 'abandonment issues' around his neck, receiving treatment and on medication – but he has his own family, home and a good job. He has grown up chronologically, intellectually, physically and, most importantly, emotionally.

Personal experience

It was a Saturday in June 2013. I awoke and put on the radio. The news was reporting that later on that day, the Queen would be attending the Trooping the Colour ceremony. As I lay there, doing nothing, the gentle drop of a faded memory soon became a flood of memories. I wasn't doing anything to distract myself or the flow of memories – pure indulgence. The emotional brain really got going, and soon I could feel a gentle wallowing taking over. I started to go through that day 30 years ago, hour by hour. I got up, washed and dressed, all on autopilot.

13 June 1981. I was going to London to meet my mother and sister. At great expense, my mother had bought tickets for the hottest show in town – a rare afternoon and evening performance of *Nicholas Nickleby*, parts 1 and 2. I left the house and a domestic crisis behind me. An adult was throwing a childish tantrum. Should I go or stay? Either way would cause more problems. I was torn.

I drove to West London, parked and got on a bus. I was still thinking about going back home. The journey slowed down as we approached Hyde Park. Of course, I had forgotten. It was Trooping the Colour today. I got off the bus in Piccadilly and wandered down Lower Regent Street towards The Mall. Crowds of people lined the road, but I found a decent position to view the procession – fortunately, I am tall.

We cheered anything and everything that went by; then the Queen rode up on her horse. No sooner had she passed than there was a commotion on the other side of the road, and the Queen's horse reared up. Police went into the crowd, but the Queen and the procession carried on. What had happened? No one knew. There was animated chatter among the crowd – then someone who had been listening to a radio said that there had been an attempt to shoot the Queen. We couldn't believe it.

I walked away and made for Charing Cross station. I needed to tell someone what I had just witnessed, and find out if the shooting story was accurate. I rang home. The reception was cool. I walked on towards the theatre, still wondering whether I should go home or stay. I felt sick. I sought out another telephone box and made a call to where my children were for the day. I still didn't feel any better, and continued walking on to the theatre. My mother and sister were there. I shared my news and also told my sister a little more of what was going on at home, but there was no turning back now.

My mother could be pedantic about the use of correct English. She questioned whether I really meant that 'the horse bolted'. I remember wanting to shout at her to shut up, but this was neither the time or place. I felt about ten years old. By now my simmering emotions were ready to boil over.

We watched the afternoon performance. I wish I could go back and really appreciate it for the tremendous theatrical production that it was. My brain was going crazy as it darted from home, the Queen and my mother to the play, even the costumes I was organising for a local amateur dramatics production in July. We then watched the evening performance, and I wondered what I would face later on: what I had I done by staying in London? I drove home. The crisis passed, for now.

Back to June 2013: I was remembering a day that is in my top ten of the most upsetting days in my life. However, for many hours I had enjoyed an outstanding theatrical performance, so it was not all bad. Bittersweet, pain and pleasure: how often does that happen? The thing is, we focus on the pain and forget the pleasure that accompanied it.

The point of wandering down this particular memory lane is to describe an emotional hijack. It came out of nowhere, and was unexpected. I did not have anything to distract me, neither did I choose to find something. It was an emotional wound, and I wanted to pick at the scab and feel the pain that I knew would occur: a type of 'self-harm'. I couldn't help the first thought, but I did have control over the second one: I chose not to leave well alone. The toxins came out. An hour later, I was left with anger – no surprise there. Fortunately, I knew what I was doing and how to deal with unhelpful emotional arousal. A few hours later, the memory and its associated emotions faded again, and this story now has become a teaching tale. I'm *retelling* it, not *reliving* it.

Illustration

My friend and colleague, Sue Hanisch, was caught in an IRA bomb blast in Victoria Station, London, on 18 February 1991. She experienced severe physical injuries, loss of a limb and severe mental trauma. She had undiagnosed post-traumatic stress disorder (PTSD). Her career as an occupational therapist was over. Her marriage was over. Her life was over – or so she believed at that time.

The Legal people were engaged. Compensation was sought through the Criminal Injury Compensation Board and dragged on for seven years. In 1998, a decision was finally made about the value of Sue's injuries. She was hugely relieved that at last there was a conclusion to the legal posturing, but felt like she had been a human pinball in a legal process.

However, what good was this award to her? Sue walked away from the court, but couldn't work out what the connection was between what had just been decided, and the rest of her life. How could the award could be related to her day-to-day life? After all, she had lived seven years hearing and believing from the doctors and lawyers: "You poor soul", "It's hopeless", "You can't dance", " You can't go in the sea", "You'll never play tennis". The negativity was endless and soul-destroying.

Sue had had to tell her story over and over again, continually picking away at the wounds, never allowing for any healing to take place. The legal profession were dabbling in Sue's wounds as well to prolong the process, so that the wound could stay open. As Sue came out of court, she felt that her life was over. Money would make little difference. Her thinking had become as disabled as her body at that time. After all, she couldn't do anything, could she? She would never be able to do anything, would she? However, there was a glimmer of hope that had not been extinguished. At some level Sue knew that sooner or later, the wheels would have to start turning again.

It took a little time, with great support from friends and some de-traumatising treatment, but Sue has gone on to achieve remarkable things in her life and continues to do so. I have been present at some of them, such as her first game of tennis. It is a privilege to count her as a friend and inspiration.

In 2013, Sue works for The Lindy Fourie Foundation in South Africa, and the Phoenix Aid Charity in Bosnia and the West Bank. She also works with children and the military in the UK.

Reflection

Autobiography in Five Chapters

Chapter 1
I walk down the street.
There is a deep hole in the pavement. I fall in.
I am lost... I am hopeless.
It isn't my fault.
It takes forever to find a way out.

Chapter 2
I walk down the same street.
There is a deep hole in the pavement.
I pretend I don't see it.
I fall in again.
I can't believe I'm in the same place.
But, it isn't my fault.
It still takes me a long time to get out.

Chapter 3
I walk down the street.
There is a deep hole in the pavement.
I see it is there.
I still fall in... It's a habit.
My eyes are open.
I know where I am.
It is my fault.
I get out immediately.

Chapter 4
I walk down the same street.
There is a deep hole in the pavement.
I walk around it.

Chapter 5
I walk down another street.

Portia Nelson

Chapter 17

'I won't!': secondary gain

If I'm not ill, will my dad still love me?

Sophie, aged 19

When I was studying for my psychotherapy diploma, there was a sizeable manual to accompany the course. Near the back, there was a section that took up one-third of the page: it was titled 'Secondary Gain'. It was a topic for discussion towards the end of the course and didn't take too long to cover. Fifteen years later, there is a consensus of opinion among many colleagues that 'secondary gain' has been the largest contributor to clients not succeeding in solving their problems in a totally satisfactory manner. I feel that much more should have been made of its consequences in therapeutic practice.

"I won't" is often a statement accompanied by a childish sulk or tantrum; certainly, some physical behaviour can be observed. I am always bemused when I see someone pouting. On the other hand, refusing to do something that has been suggested by someone else can be a good idea. The peer pressure felt by young people to do something that perhaps they are not comfortable with cannot be ignored. As I write, at the beginning of 2013, there is much publicity about the pressure young girls are experiencing to take part in 'sexting': sending texts and films of themselves in sexual poses or performing sexual acts to a boy or man. This is an unhealthy way to feel needed, accepted and thought 'good enough'. In states of heightened arousal and possible emotional manipulation, both children and adults fail to comprehend the long term consequenses of posting photos, which can stay on line for ever.

What is secondary gain?

Secondary gain occurs when a person acknowledges that there is a problem to be solved, but is not willing to give up a behaviour that they have developed as part of the solution. At the top of the secondary gain list is financial gain. It is tempting: why change if it may mean a financial loss in some way? In my experience, the top of the financial gain list is a tie between welfare benefits and insurance claims. I started to take insurance cases but, in the end, I refused to for ethical reasons. I advertised as a short-term therapist, which meant that I usually saw people for between two and six appointments. After a time, I realised that the secondary gain of having an insurance claim meant that the motivation to get better, and not have the problem arising from the accident, was missing. I could have carried on, but as satisfaction in my work came from helping people change their lives, I found the work a struggle.

Some of my colleagues now question the use of the word 'benefit', wondering if it really is a benefit for everyone who receives it. Does it encourage a 'won't do/can't do' society? This is not political, it is based on experience. Certainly, claiming benefits is the other area of financial gain that I have observed in holding people back from making some beneficial changes in their lives.

It is the same for illnesses and chronic conditions. You may have come across cases of two people who have similar chronic conditions: they may have similar backgrounds and living conditions. But while one person will be working, holding down a job, keeping a career going and running a home and social life; for the other person, the chronic condition becomes their very existence, their reason to be. Attempting to minimise the discomfort and problems that the condition presents are anathema to them: they won't.

There are other gains to be made by 'refusing' behaviour.

Getting attention

If the problem being presented succeeds in getting people's attention, then why change it? We have a genuine need to give and receive attention. If sulking and tantrums succeed in giving a person what they want, they are likely to continue. The same can happen with illnesses. "If I'm not ill, will my dad still love me?" said Sophie, who knew that she was creating health problems where they may not have existed. However, she had become genuinely unwell as a little girl. At the same time, her younger sibling was born – she knew what she was doing, and acknowledged it. She decided to grow up and became a healthy young woman.

Phobias

Phobias are genuine, and a phobic reaction can be most unpleasant and frightening. However, they can be cured. The problem is that avoidance tactics may have been developed over the years to manage them: it can seem not worth giving up the phobia in order to tackle daily tasks such as the shopping, a social activity, childcare or family visiting.

Keeping hold of old belief systems

As children we can make some dogmatic statements: "Because I never have" "Because I can't/won't." My personal favourites were "I will never eat tomatoes" and "I will never wear a skirt over my knees again". How limited my life would have been, had I kept those two beliefs. We can hold on to childhood beliefs because we have never had to challenge ourselves to change. (Mind you, I am still dogmatic about one thing, many decades later: "I will never drink tea". Horrible stuff – and I have tried, I promise you!)

Attitude is key

We can change. From childhood we have changed our age, our physical appearance, our intellectual capacity. We may have changed families, friends, location, jobs and hobbies. We can change our behaviour. We can change our attitude.

Personal experience

In the 1990s I was studying addiction and came across a questionnaire that people were asked to complete. The questions fascinated me. It was the first time I had ever seen anything that related to my own life events. Out of curiosity, I mentally filled the form in for myself. I was shocked. I scored considerably higher than people considered for treatment. I said to a friend, Maureen, with me, "I don't understand this. With the score on this form, I should be a patient, not a therapist. Why aren't I?"

Maureen ran her thumb down her spine and said, "Backbone". I disagreed and knew that wasn't quite right, but didn't know what the real answer was.

A few years later I came across the following passage and knew what the difference was:

The longer I live, the more I realise the impact of attitude on life. Attitude, to me, is more important than facts. It is more important than the past, than education, than money, than circumstances, than failures, than successes, than what other people think or say or do. It is more important than appearance, giftedness or skill. It will make or break a company... a church... a home. The remarkable thing is we have a choice every day regarding the attitude we will embrace for that day. We cannot change our past... we cannot change the fact that people will act in a certain way. We cannot change the inevitable. The only thing we can do is play on the one string we have, and that is our attitude... I am convinced that life is 10% what happens to me and 90% how I react to it. And so it is with you... we are in charge of our attitudes.

Charles R. Swindoll

There is a newspaper columnist called Liz Jones. She writes well and has won awards for her columns. She is also a woman who has had a number of problems managing a healthy lifestyle and life events. Many years ago, I recognised in her someone whose behaviour I would call that of 'chasing rainbows'. In my opinion, she spends her life looking to the future to bring her resolution of past injustices and makes some bizarre life choices. Whether she can help herself is not the point. The point is that, despite her multiple insecurities, would she really be interested in sorting herself out? One day I would love to meet her and find out. My thoughts are that having such an eventful life earns Liz Jones a considerable amount of money, which is good, because even with her heart in the right place she appears to leap from one financial crisis to another. While I am sure that she genuinely would like a calmer, happier life, if she achieved one, would it earn her attention and money?

I have met a number of students of different ages, who never quite managed to finish their degrees. If they were in a horse race, it would be like refusing the last fence. There are often good and valid reasons, but the secondary gain of being a student and not experiencing life on the other side of the fence can sometimes seem safer. This can be achieved by asking for extensions, taking sick leave and changing courses.

If needs such as security, finances, accommodation, friends and support are being met, then it is very tempting to stay with what you know. However, while this may be temporarily comforting, it can delay long-term growth. In a completely different environment, prison can offer similar security and needs being met.

A change of attitude can change our life. It really is worth taking a risk.

Personal experience

When writing about personal stories and events for this book, examples have readily come to mind, but not for this chapter. What behaviour do I have or can I recognise that might have led to secondary gain? Well, I procrastinate – severely. I get quite a lot done because I am always flitting from job to job, although, if I am honest, there is a downside to a butterfly mind, and that is poor productivity: loads of unfinished jobs, which drives me mad.

I am not quite sure why I procrastinate. I always have done. There are a multitude of possible reasons. Who knows? A combination perhaps. I have thought long and hard about this – "I've always been like that" could be a good reason, but it sounds like an excuse.

As a believer that unhelpful behaviours can be rooted in childhood, I have tried some introspection. My mother believed in perfectionism: anything less was not tolerated very well. I can recall playing post offices as a little girl; there was a toy cheque book and I wrote in it, in my own childish scribble. My mother wanted to show me how to write one properly. I didn't want it written properly. I was reprimanded. Christmas thank-you letters were torture.

The reasons for procrastination are numerous, but I can recognise the reason for self-sabotage in myself. It can be wrapped up in the term 'fear of the unknown'. In the same way, people who appear to fall at the last fence in college and university courses can be fearful of the future: stepping away from the security of studying and the known, into the unknown and insecurity, can be terrifying. It should be exciting and a development, but for some the fear prevents them from growing.

I am reminded of something I used to read to clients sometimes when they were deeply relaxed, and their unconscious would allow the words to sink in:

Our deepest fear is not that we are inadequate. Our deepest fear is that we are powerful beyond measure. It is our light, not our darkness that most frightens us. We ask ourselves, who am I to be brilliant, gorgeous, talented, fabulous? Actually, who are you not to be? You are a child of God. Your playing small does not serve the world. There is nothing enlightened about shrinking so that other people won't feel insecure around you. We are all meant to shine, as children do. We were born to make manifest the glory of God that is within us. It's not just in some of us; it's in everyone. And as we let our own light shine, we unconsciously give other people permission to do the same. As we are liberated from our own fear, our presence automatically liberates others.

Marianne Williamson

Who benefits?

David Servan-Schreiber was co-founder and then director of the Centre for Integrative Medicine at the University of Pittsburgh. He wrote the popular book, *Healing without Freud or Prozac* (see Bibliography). I recall reading about a clinic that he had opened using his methods. It had to close for financial reasons. If clients can improve in a short time, how many do you have to have to make a clinic viable? I can report that short-term therapy does not make for a good business model: my practice was thriving with clients but the only time I was in profit was when I was working for a local authority with guaranteed clients and income. Therapists often have to look at other ways of supplementing their income, such as running workshops, lecturing, writing and supervising.

Illustration

There are temptations for therapists to prolong treatment. Richard came to see me. He had been to another therapist locally, who kept on saying, "We've nearly got to it, just one more session." Richard had had around 30 sessions. This therapist also used to tell him about the wonderful time he was having with his private plane.

As part of my diploma training, we were given warnings about dependency. Dependency arising from getting personal needs met through the client/therapist dynamic. Dependency that can work both ways.

PTSD among service personnel is rightly getting more headlines than it used to: it is sad to think that this disturbing condition was unrecognised in both World Wars, with devastating results. In fact it is still under-diagnosed. There are several organisations that can help: SSAFA, Combat Stress and PTSD Resolution among them. However, places for the Combat Stress programme are fewer than the number of applicants, so getting a place can be difficult.

Illustration

An ex-soldier came to see me. Jed showed all the symptoms of PTSD and was waiting for a place on the Combat Stress programme. He needed and wanted help, but something was holding him back from accepting the de-traumatising help that I could offer him. If he got better, he wouldn't need his place on the Combat Stress programme: the place was precious, and counted for something with the Benefits Agency. When I saw Jed for his second appointment, he was showing signs of improvement. He knew that he felt better too. So he stopped seeing me – he couldn't face the risk of losing his place on the Combat Stress programme, and told me that this was the reason to stop seeing me.

Reflection

Is there a behaviour or life choice that you would like to change?

Write down the behaviour or life choice.

What are the benefits from keeping this behaviour or life choice?

Do you gain attention? Friendship? Money? Work?

Do you really want to change?

Chapter 18

'I can't help it': choices

> *We need to teach the next generation of children from day one that they are responsible for their lives. Mankind's greatest gift, also its greatest curse, is that we have free choice. We can make our choices built from love or from fear.*
>
> **Elisabeth Kübler-Ross**

Some people don't like the expression "You've got a choice". In fact, some people hate being told that they have choices – it places the responsibility for their actions squarely with themselves.

However, in some parts of our lives perhaps we have too much choice. I was in the supermarket looking at the numerous varieties of coffee on the shelves. Another woman was looking too. I said, "I remember the day when it was a choice between Nescafe or Maxwell House." She laughed: "That's so true. I've just spent five minutes in front of the stock cubes." Is there too much choice? Do we waste time making choices?

Childrearing goes through fashions. The more recent, liberal theory is that children should be given choices rather than directed: for example, "What T shirt would you like to put on?", "What would you like to eat?" I am not sure that this is always very helpful; a little direction, which saves time and a small child's uncertainty, may be for the best. When running the toddler group, if I had allowed the two-year-olds to make those kinds of choices it would have led to chaos.

The power of advertising

The child's brain develops fast, but emotional development lags behind other areas of development. There is often an emotional element to our choices, although generally we are not aware of it. I am amazed that some people disagree with this statement. Without the emotional element that comes into making choices, the advertising business would be dead. Music and images sell. Children are known for 'pester power'. Children see, hear and want. Adults also see, hear and may want, but the brain is more mature and they can stop before taking action – can't they? Not always.

Learning about memory-matching and how it can lead to subsequent thoughts and behaviours has been a revelation. I am fascinated by how advertisers, marketing and media use these neural connections. Our brains are full of millions of images taken from our lives. Imagine the brain as the biggest photo album in the world. Now, take a pleasant image and add a smell. Add a sound, maybe add a taste. Savour the image. Feel the emotion that arises. The memory has taken hold and could be triggered by a similar sight, sound, smell or taste.

Illustration

I was in the cinema with Polly, who had never had children. The advertisements before the film were full of ones for cars, as usual. After one such advert, Polly said, "That's just silly. Why do they use those stupid voices?" I told her that they were from a favourite TV children's cartoon from the 1980s about racing cars, called *Wacky Races*. The advert wasn't aimed at the over-fifties, like us, it was for 30 to 40-year-olds. Clever marketing.

I am the same age as Twiggy, an 'older' model for Marks & Spencer (sadly, that is our only similarity). The imagery of her modelling heyday in the 1960s is still there in her face. No wonder M&S use her – she was worth millions to the company. But I was relieved when I saw Twiggy on a TV programme and could see some lines on her face. The dreaded airbrush was missing. No wonder young people are so influenced by airbrushed images.

The soundtrack behind adverts, smells in supermarkets, the use of famous personalities, clever words, carefully chosen images – the list is endless. Match the image to a positive experience that a customer has had somewhere in their lives, and you may have a sale. This is why nostalgia sells so well. However, a purchase bought with expectations arising from a memory may well disappoint, as it can never be exactly the same.

If an advertiser cannot match to a positive experience, then it can promise something better for the customer: something that will make them feel better in their community, something that will make them feel better about themselves. One detergent company spent many years suggesting that the worst thing you could do for your child was send them to school wearing a shirt that wasn't as white as the child's who lived next door. The woman was obviously a terrible mother, who was made not to feel good enough. The soap powder became the brand leader. I can remember, back in 1971, my neighbour mentioning how another neighbour's nappies hanging on the line weren't so white.

All manipulation. All mind games. Everybody's mind and their choices worth billions of pounds.

Visualising the solution

A client, Jan, said to me, "I don't know why I came to see you really, I knew where I had to go next." I replied, "A map is only useful if you know where you are in the first place and you didn't. Now you do."

When I was in practice, I used the natural trance states of relaxation and hypnotic techniques to help the client absorb information. Often, if the client's problems were about decisions and choices I would read this poem – they always enjoyed it. There is a bestselling self-help book, *The Road Less Travelled*, by the psychiatrist M. Scott Peck, named after it.

The Road Not Taken

Two roads diverged in a yellow wood,
And sorry I could not travel both
And be one traveler, long I stood
And looked down one as far as I could
To where it bent in the undergrowth;

Then took the other, as just as fair,
And having perhaps the better claim,
Because it was grassy and wanted wear;
Though as for that the passing there
Had worn them really about the same,

And both that morning equally lay
In leaves no feet had trodden black.
Oh, I kept the first for another day!
Yet knowing how way leads on to way,
I doubted if I should ever come back.

I shall be telling this with a sigh
Somewhere ages and ages hence:

Two roads diverged in a wood, and I –
I took the one less traveled by,
And that has made all the difference.

Robert Frost

Using visual perspective in a relaxation exercise can help to achieve clarity when trying to resolve a problem and making choices. For example, if you have ever been lost in a forest – and I have – it can be very frightening. Every turn looks similar and, when there is cloud cover means you cannot tell where the sun is. If you adopt a bird's eye view, the way out becomes clear. The view is usually better from the top of the tree than the bottom. When Ed Peppitt of *Balloon View* publishing agreed to publish this book, I thought the synchronicity just perfect.

It can be more effective to illustrate a point using something visual. If humour and live action can be brought into the proceedings, all the better, as the person being guided is likely to remember something unusual. At times I used my practice room to illustrate points, if it felt like a helpful action to take. I can remember pushing the door shut against intrusive thoughts, walking round the room through timelines, and using a dying plant that wasn't having its needs met. Illustrating a lack of perspective on a problem was my favourite.

Illustration

Tricia had a problem. It loomed large in her life. There was no way round it, under it or over it. I stood up, moved to the closed door and pressed my face onto the door. I said, "This is my problem. I can't get out of the room. I'm stuck and can't see any solutions, so I'm panicking." I looked very silly, with my face pressed hard on the door, so Tricia started to laugh, which helped break her emotional state.

I moved one step back and saw a door handle. One choice.

I took another step back and saw a window. Two choices.

I moved another step back and saw a telephone, which I could use to get help. Three choices.

Three choices, where previously there had been none. It is easy when you are able to step back and think logically and rationally.

Personal experience

Sue Hanisch and I were in Australia. Together with colleagues, we were running workshops in Victoria, New South Wales and Queensland. We had a great time and I don't think I have ever laughed so much in my life. One evening, Sue and I were enjoying an evening meal and a glass of wine on a hotel terrace in a coastal resort. A storm was brewing, and thunder could be heard in the distance. I used to be petrified of thunderstorms, but through helping clients with thunder phobias, I have appeared to help myself. I still don't like them, but can tolerate them. Sue had been badly injured in an IRA bomb at London's Victoria Station in 1991 (see Chapter 16). While her post-traumatic stress disorder had been successfully treated, understandably she still jumped at loud bangs and bright flashes.

We ate our meal and drank the wine, thoroughly enjoying each other's company. It started to rain, but it was warm, we were under cover and so stayed on the terrace. The thunderstorm steadily built in its intensity. It was slightly frightening but exciting too, as the skies and trees lit up with the lightning. We talked about a technique for lowering emotional arousal, called the Emotional Freedom Technique (EFT). Later on we both trained in the technique, but all we knew at that point was that it somehow involved tapping on the face, head and various parts of the upper body. It seemed a bit silly to us at the time, and encouraged giggling.

The storm started to become tropical. We looked around. We were sitting outside the large dining room window: there were diners inside. The doors to the hotel were a little way away and not under cover. If we tried to go inside, we would get wet, so we stayed outside. We consumed more wine. The rain became harder, the thunder louder. Our chatting became a little more high-pitched and more giggly. We started to tap away at our faces in a slightly hysterical way. We moved closer together as the rain encroached on the terrace.

Eventually, with Sue and I nearly on top of one another, we knew we were going to have to make a run for it and get drenched. I looked around at the diners again, through the large glass window. This time I noticed the window frame: There was a handle. The window wasn't a window – it was a patio door.

We opened it and went inside. The diners said, "Oh, we thought you wanted to stay out there." I don't think we did anything for the reputation of crazy Poms.

Emotional arousal (and alcohol) had made us stupid and unable to see our choices.

Most of the time we cannot control the first thought that comes into our head because it is random, but we can take control over the second and subsequent. When I took out a Yellow Pages advertisement in 2002, I suggested to the salesperson that they looked at my website for information. The next time I spoke to her, she said, "I found your website most illuminating. It has never occurred to me that I could change my thoughts." Wow! What a powerful insight. Could that mean that a large proportion of the population are also unaware of the choices they have over their emotions, thoughts and subsequent behaviours?

Reflection

When we are children, we generally believe what our 'olders and betters' tell us. Sometimes there are good and fun reasons to be told something: for example, Father Christmas, fairies taking lost teeth, or pots of gold at the end of the rainbow.

However, we grow up and see, hear or read the evidence, and change our minds. If we are emotionally healthy, we leave behind the childhood beliefs if they aren't helpful. We take on new beliefs – we grow up emotionally.

Here is a useful tool to challenge your beliefs, if they are leading to unhelpful choices being made.

Ask yourself these questions.

1. Did you ever believe in the tooth fairy?

2. If so, who told you it existed?

3. Do you believe in the tooth fairy now?

4. How old were you when you learned the truth about the tooth fairy?

5. What evidence made you change your mind?

Now change some words: remove 'the tooth fairy' from the above sentences, and replace it with your own limiting beliefs.

1. Did you ever believe that you were: unloved, unwanted,

friendless, hopeless, stupid, a failure, no good, useless or any other negative descriptions attributed to you? (Basically, words or deeds that you believed, and left you with a feeling that you were not good enough in some way.)

2. Who used these descriptions about you first?

3. Did that person really know you?

4. In what context were they used? Look at the whole picture.

5. Do you think they are still relevant today?

6. If you do, why? What is the evidence?

7. Could you put away those childhood memories of negativity and recall times when there is evidence to show that these statements are now inaccurate?

8. If not, why not?

Chapter 19

'Why should I?': self-awareness

> *What is necessary to change a person is to change their awareness of themselves.*
>
> **Abraham Maslow**

When children reach a certain stage in their development, they start to become aware of their surroundings and begin asking questions: "Why?" There are few parents who have not become exasperated by the sometimes continual questioning. Some of the questions just do not have an answer beyond "because it does". Some don't have an answer at all, and we can gaze at the child in exasperation as they demand an answer to an impossible question.

At a toddler group I ran for two-year-olds, we were singing *Humpty Dumpty*: "Humpty Dumpty sat on the wall, Humpty Dumpty had a great fall." Before I could begin the next line, a little boy's voice piped up: "Why?" "Why what?" I asked. "Why did he fall off the wall?" Good question.

However, if by the end of this book, anything written in it rings a few bells or presses a few buttons, why shouldn't you stop and think? Is there something you do that could be found irritating? Something that causes a problem for someone else? Perhaps there is something that goes so far as to cause distress and unhappiness, both to you and others. Why carry on with a behaviour that causes problems?

> **Example**
>
> Mandy recognised that part of her 38-year-old self was behaving like a seven-year-old. I suggested that it might feel like she was wearing an adult shoe on one foot and a child's shoe on the other. "My goodness," she exclaimed, as the realisation came to her, "I've been limping through my life."
>
> It is interesting that one of the phrases used to express frustration at someone's behaviour is "Act your age, not your shoe size!" The remedy was in Mandy's hands. It was her responsibility to adjust her thinking and behaviour in that particular area of life.

'Why should I? I'm not harming anyone'

All our interactions will have some effect somewhere along the line. If someone cannot be bothered to attend to their well-being, then the consequences will affect their nearest and dearest, their work colleagues, and possibly take up valuable time and space in the NHS, depriving someone else of that time and space. People in denial will be unaware that their denial is causing problems to other people they are in contact with.

We need to have a level of self-awareness for healthy relationships. This can be a most challenging area. I do not always succeed: it needs a few moments for reflection, and that is not always available.

Illustration

Jaz came to the city to see his daughter settled in at university. We all met in the city centre, and I took them to a cafe in one of the wonderful back streets. My heart sunk a little when I saw the waitress, as she tends to welcome guests a bit too loudly and fulsomely; however, the cafe is quirky and the food is great, so I always think it is worth a visit. The waitress took the order from Jaz's 21-year-old daughter, then referred me to the young woman as "your mother". We all laughed. I am old enough to be the young woman's grandmother, and Jaz is more than a decade younger than me. Not an impossible arrangement, I agree, but totally wrong in this case.

It is easy to make assumptions but, as we mature, we attempt to learn to 'engage brain before opening mouth'. I am sure we can all think of times that we have spoken first without thinking – and rather wish we hadn't. In these times of social media, equally it could be: 'Engage brain before opening mouth – or texting, tweeting or writing on Facebook.'

Personal experience

Roger went to the funeral of the wife of a man of local importance. The funeral was well attended, due to the respect shown to the man. His wife had been a challenging woman. The vicar spoke and mentioned that the woman had held strong opinions, before he paused, as if it was difficult to find the right words. Then he said, "and she had lovely hair".

Not long after Roger told me this story, I went to visit my aunt in California. She was nearly 90 and lived in a very pleasant gated community, of which there are many in the USA. I attended church with her on Sunday: there were about 200 people present, the average age being around 75, and the preacher was a Mr De'Ath. The sermon was based on the reading which, curiously enough, had been about death. I wondered what he was going to say. He was straightforward: he discussed how people were going to be talked about at their funerals – should they change anything about themselves that might not be very nice? It was very thought-provoking. I remembered Roger's experience.

Self-awareness and materialism

When pictures are in the media after natural disasters, such as tsunamis, hurricanes or tornadoes, all that is to be seen is devastation and loss. Thousands of people left with nothing, sometimes even with no family, but mostly without even their basic needs. It makes me wonder: if you take everything away, you are only left with yourself. If your view of yourself is based only on material wealth and status, how do you manage your recovery?

I came into this world with nothing, and I will leave with nothing but love. Everything else is just borrowed.

Ed Sheeran

Seeing ourselves clearly

Jason told me that he didn't have any friends. Bold, black and white statements always should be gently challenged. He told me that, for example, he was a regular at the pub and everyone avoided him. He was unable to think of a reason why they did – or at least why they were not expressing it. I asked Jason to take an imaginary trip to the pub with me. I suggested that as we walk through the doors, we see him sitting at the bar: "He looks a decent enough bloke, why don't we go over and join him?" I said. The response was a fierce "No!" I asked Jason why we shouldn't join him at the bar. He replied that he was a bastard who tried to steal his mates' girlfriends. Now there was something tangible to discuss.

If we do not use this personal resource, we may continue to behave in ways that produce unhelpful results, meanwhile blaming others. Einstein is attributed as giving this definition of insanity: "Doing the same thing over and over again, and expecting different results." Or, as it is said these days: "If you always do what you've always done, you'll always get what you've always got."

There is one crucial element that stops us seeing ourselves: a state of emotional arousal. Our line of vision becomes so narrow and the brain so cut off from reality, that being able to use our rational viewfinder is impossible. We become myopic. Realisation sometimes arrives in 'the cold light of day', when we look back with horror at something that we wish we hadn't done. The reverse can be true too. We 'sleep on it' and in the morning not only can our problem not appear so all consuming, but solutions may readily come to the rested mind.

If you want something to change, start viewing.

Reflection

One of the resources that helps human beings with problem-solving is the ability to be able to observe themselves. This has been called the 'observing self', and acts like a internal CCTV camera where we can imagine ourselves looking at our own behaviour. (We should note that I am not talking about disassociation here; there are a number of writings about people who speak of near-death experiences, feeling that they are floating on the ceiling while looking down on their own body being attended to by medical staff. Certainly, we are aware that in traumatic circumstances, people report being able to take themselves out of their body to protect themselves. There is very likely to be a neurological connection, but that is outside the scope of this book.)

Being our own 'fly on the wall' can be uncomfortable at times, but very helpful for reflection and personal understanding. Suddenly seeing a reflection of ourselves in a mirror or shop window can be an unpleasant surprise at times – as we age, it does not seem to get any better. It may be that we become aware that we are standing too close to someone and they are feeling uncomfortable. Perhaps we are speaking too loudly, or listening to a music player too loudly. Have you ever thought what you might look like, having had too much to drink? Perhaps you are too dominant in meetings?

People who can recognise that they are acting like 'a spoilt brat', 'a little princess' or 'a five-year-old', are all using their observing self. However, beware! This kind of observation is not about self-reflection of a negative type, for example: "I'm such a failure", "I'm hopeless", and so forth. Like the man in the pub, this sort of statement needs a little investigation.

Ask yourself these questions.

> What is the evidence?
> Who says?
> Is that personal belief past its sell-by date?

Use the emotional growth chart in Appendix 4.

The emotional growth chart is a chart I designed as an illustration of how our mini-me can prevent healthy emotional growth.

1. In the Past column, write the age/ages of your mini-me.

If you are honest with yourself, you will be able to identify how old you feel when childish behaviours intrude into adult life.

Write down any life-limiting beliefs and missing emotional needs you feel you had at the time. "I wasn't good enough because..."

2. In the Present column, write your age now.

Write down your strengths, abilities and skills. If it's a struggle, think of your CV.

3. In Ongoing choices, write down some new, life-changing choices that you are going to make.

4. Complete another chart in three months, six months, a year's time and look for improvements in your life.

This chart came from a doodle to show a client what was happening in his life. As we worked along the emotional timeline, he was able to identify times when his mini-me had hijacked him through life and he felt taken back to the past age. As the hijack loops built up, we became aware that we had drawn a rainbow.

Chapter 20

'Leave me alone': the need for privacy

> *Being solitary is being alone well: being alone luxuriously immersed in doings of your own choice, aware of the fullness of your won presence rather than of the absence of others. Because solitude is an achievement.*
>
> **Alice Koller**

Privacy, or time on one's own, is like the refrain in the story of 'Goldilocks and the Three Bears'. Too much is not right. Too little is not right. We need a balance of just enough to be just right. However, in reality, who is able to achieve that? We are just as likely to be screaming inside that we want to be alone for just a minute, as we are feeling that we are getting too much of our own company.

I had a crazily busy life that veered from barely a moment alone, to one where every evening was spent on my own with the TV and red wine for company – but I did discover the difference between loneliness and solitude. I spent many hours feeling very solitary but, due to a great network of family and friends, I never felt lonely.

We can look at other people's lives and think they have something that we don't. Jenny, who was unable to have children, went to visit some friends in America. There was an outing to a busy local picnic spot. Her friend, Paula, had young children who were fairly rowdy. At the end of the day, Paula was exhausted and told Jenny that all she could see in the park were childless couples having fun. Jenny remarked that all she could see were happy families with children.

Personal experience

Many people have said that Sundays are the most difficult day to manage on one's own. I have experienced both the delight of a Sunday to myself and the emptiness too. One particular holiday weekend was difficult for me, and I forced myself to go out. I visited a beautiful city, but it didn't seem so beautiful that day as it was full of families on holiday. I went shopping, but not very enthusiastically. By chance, I bumped into some friends, who invited me back to the boat that they had hired on the river. I enjoyed a couple of hours in their company, and felt a twinge of envy at their happy family and comfortable lifestyle. A few years later they had divorced – all was not what it seemed.

I would add that the memory reminds me that the whole weekend was fairly a miserable one. There were difficult realisations to accept and I can laugh about it now, but at 43 I thought I was heading towards an unknown and uncertain retirement. However, within a month my whole life had changed for the better in a most unexpected way. My fifties were stuffed with unimagined and extraordinary experiences, and my sixties are so far pretty good too. As the saying goes: "it's better than the alternative".

A room of one's own

I remember visiting my godmother, Pamela. She was a painter and writer. In later life she had married again: an older man who was a retired ship's captain. I went to visit them in their house and was a little surprised at how characterless it felt – a few pieces of brown furniture and some fairly dull furnishings. She had been such a lively woman with three children, but this house felt less welcoming than her previous home. Then we went upstairs and she showed me a bedroom which she had turned into a workroom. It was like watching a black and white movie that turns into technicolour: chintz ruled, and I understood. The main house was to her husband's liking, and maybe as a former captain he was used to small and functional areas. My aunt had her own space which she had arranged to her own liking. It was a working compromise.

Sheds, garages, cubbyholes under the stairs, spare bedrooms – they all achieve the same purpose. A space that can be called one's own. If that is out of the question, then an activity that one can call one's own can work as well. Not that we want this all the time, however loneliness and isolation are attracting the attention of the media. Many people keep themselves to themselves and do not join in with community; there are also more single people and lone parent families.

A positive approach to time out

I do believe that we have to help ourselves, and that is where emotional maturity plays its part. As children, our lives are organised and run by adults, but as adults we should not expect other people to provide our entertainment. I came across a letter to an agony aunt recently: a woman in her sixties bemoaning her feeling of isolation. The agony aunt suggested that the woman try to be more proactive about seeking out company and taking up activities, and less negative about her situation. The woman had expressed self-pity and feelings of unfairness, and this would not help her to move forward. I felt concerned that unless the woman changed her attitude, then her future was unlikely to improve.

The thing is, for some people, their own company is uncomfortable. It can lead to introspection of the 'If you pick it, it won't get better' variety. Some people dislike themselves enough to want to avoid being in their own company, while others people think that taking some time out for themselves is selfish: it means that they are lazy.

Illustration

Sheila was exhausted. She had retired and worked for a local church. Despite pleas from friends to take some time out and enjoy her retirement, she was unable to – she expressed feelings of fear at doing nothing, and felt driven to be busy every day. Not only busy, but doing work that was not frivolous.

What was her driving force? A negative voice from decades before, drowning out the common-sense voice to rest. When Sheila was at school, she was caught in a cupboard, messing around with friends. The headteacher opened the door and shouted at them, in no uncertain terms: "Don't ever let me see you doing nothing ever again!" Despite being over 70, Sheila had not been able to put that incident into context and make up her own mind, using her logical brain.

Be kind to yourself

"Treat yourself kindly": this is something I used to prescribe sometimes, especially for those experiencing bereavement. I used to be surprised at how many people needed permission from a professional to take some time out: "Best advice I was given", a client told me.

When I was experiencing a self-inflicted meltdown in the workplace (see Chapter 4), I carried on and made matters worse when a short period of sick leave would have helped – that came later, and was almost too late. I had thought that going sick was a weakness. It wouldn't have been – it would have been a strength.

Thinking time. Being still. Putting things into perspective. Certainly some problem-solving can be achieved in states of high emotional arousal in an emergency, but generally if we want to look at all the options available to us, we need the mind to be more relaxed so that the brain can work effectively. Using alcohol and drugs is a common way of relaxing and switching-off the noise of life, but they come with a price: addiction and/or later problems with ill-health. In the same way that as children we were often given a sweet or biscuit to 'make it better' when we had hurt ourselves, rewarding stress and a need to relax with alcohol and drugs sends a message to our brain that this is what we do when we need to relax.

Personal experience

My mother once told me that she stopped drinking whisky on a work night to relax because she felt that it could lead to increased consumption. I didn't really understand until, many years later, I found myself in a situation where an after-work drink was all too easy to consume, followed by another one. The frustration of never being able to watch an evening TV drama without falling asleep, and then having a dreadful night's sleep, eventually won over the need for a drink on arriving home. Even now, the bottle of red wine can be too handy to 'make it better' – but I choose other ways to relax. A warm bubble bath and some good music can be a nice alternative, even if it does take a little more effort.

Why is privacy important?

"Stop the world, I want to get off!" is something I find myself thinking sometimes, as my world seems to whirl out of control. As I get older I have also become increasingly aware of the phrases "Be careful what you wish for" and "self-fulfilling prophecy". An afternoon left to one's own devices may seem attractive, but a week, month or even a year of being on one's own may not seem so attractive.

When we are with people, what role are we playing? I wrote these notes after experiencing a particularly varied week of activities.

Monday: I'm me. Also a wife. I'm at home writing, so the day is mine, except for the bit of admin I have to do for a group I belong to – so I'll add 'club member'.

Tuesday: I attended a workshop on 'anger', part of continuing professional development. I could say the day has been totally just about me, the writer, but I've met some colleagues, so wore that hat too. I went to London to my son's house, whereupon I'm 'mum' when the children are in bed, and 'mad granny' when they are up.

Wednesday: A day with my grandson, so full-on granny role. A friend too – we visit a lifelong friend who is also on half-term duty with her nephew and nieces.

Thursday: Meet husband at station. Travel to south coast for sister-in-law's funeral. Wife, aunt and great-aunt.

Friday: Same county, but inland to visit my mother; husband joins me later. So, wife and daughter.

Saturday: A surprise retirement party for brother-in-law: sister, sister-in-law, wife and acquaintance.

Sunday: Neighbour pops in for regular Sunday morning coffee and chat.

I would agree that the week contained a few one-off life events, and so was slightly unusual, but you can see the point. In order to write, you cannot let anyone else in, so not much writing was done that week. It couldn't be helped, but I felt a bit of resentment. I needed a bit of 'me time'. When I had the children at home, I craved time just to read the newspaper – that was my 'me time', and if I didn't get it, I could get irritated. I not only wanted it, I actually needed it.

That need is one that we all have at times: some 'me time', some space. It is not about being selfish, it is about allowing the brain to slow down. A time to rest the mind and body. A time to recharge the batteries. Like the battery indicator on a mobile phone, we all need to have a time for our mind and body to recharge, otherwise our batteries run out. We are warned. Our body tells us, the red light goes on – and we don't listen to our cost. Or perhaps our mind and body feel like an electrical socket, and each demand on us is a plug: it is easy to imagine how the circuit can be overloaded. We need to remove a plug or two, or just switch off the whole system for a while.

Example

Sally wrote about her husband having to go away on business: "It's been wonderful to have a break from each other. I've really enjoyed it, though I'm noticing the lack of companionship and stimulus provided by someone else's company."

It reminded me of the retired woman's motto: "I married you for life, but not for lunch".

As with so many things in life, this is a case of balance: not too little, and not too much. There are too many people, especially the elderly, experiencing too much 'me time' and feeling isolated.

Reflection

This poem is about time out: time for thinking, time for perspective.

Leisure

What is this life if, full of care,
We have no time to stand and stare.

No time to stand beneath the boughs
And stare as long as sheep or cows.

No time to see, when woods we pass,
Where squirrels hide their nuts in grass.

No time to see, in broad daylight,
Streams full of stars, like skies at night.

No time to turn at Beauty's glance,
And watch her feet, how they can dance.

No time to wait till her mouth can
Enrich that smile her eyes began.

A poor life this if, full of care,
We have no time to stand and stare.

William Henry Davies

Relaxation techniques

Tools such as relaxation techniques and massage are more effective if they are used early: for example, before a person's arousal level becomes too high. High arousal requires more effort to achieve a result, but if we are tired, stressed or under the influence of alcohol and drugs, we can find it more difficult.

The secret is to practise these techniques when you are not feeling stressed or out of control, then they will come more easily when you need to use them. The correct breathing will slow your heart rate, which in turn lowers your pulse and your blood pressure. Taking the breath down into the centre of your body provides your internal organs with more oxygen, so helping to release the accumulated stresses that can build up, causing damage (see Appendix 3).

When you read Appendix 3, you may realise that many smokers feel a benefit from smoking because of the calming effect that their breathing action is having on them, rather than the power of nicotine.

Summary
The end... or just the beginning?

We live in the past or in the future; we are continually expecting the coming of some special moment when our life will unfold itself in its full significance. And we do not notice that life is flowing like water through our fingers.

Father Alexander Elchanov

There are three groups of people who read summaries, so I will write three summaries.

Group 1: Readers who have read the whole book.

I hope that this book delivered what it said on the cover. You have read about my own personal insights and been given some practical insights. You should now be full of your own insights, perhaps about some of your own behaviours: are you sure you don't recognise yourself somewhere? If not, then certainly those of people you know in your family, socially, workplace and the wider world. It could lead to some life-changing decisions.

Group 2: Readers who have dipped into different chapters.

I hope you were tempted by the chapter headings. Did you find what you were looking for? If you didn't, carry on and read the whole book. It will be worth it.

Group 3: Readers who have turned to the summaries to see whether the book is worth reading at all.

It is. There are insights that will be thought-provoking, inspire discussion and may even change your life. If you're not sure about reading it all, start with the Preface, Introduction, Chapters 1, 2 and 11.

"When one door of happiness closes, another opens; but often we look so long at the closed door that we do not see the one which has been opened for us."

Helen Keller

Appendix 1:
Hemispheres of the brain

Brain Functions

Right Hemisphere

Emotional Expression

Fight or Flight

Spacial Awareness

Music

Creativity

Imagination

Dimension

Left Hemisphere

Writing

Languages

Science

Mathematics

Lists

Logic

Analysis

Appendix 2: Soroptimists International bookmark

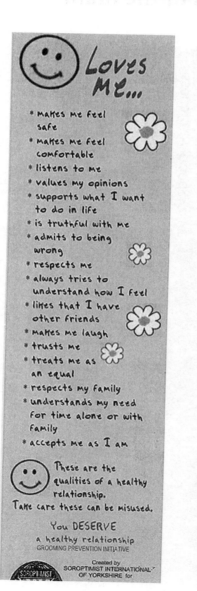

Loves Me...

* makes me feel safe
* makes me feel comfortable
* listens to me
* values my opinions
* supports what I want to do in life
* is truthful with me
* admits to being wrong
* respects me
* always tries to understand how I feel
* likes that I have other friends
* makes me laugh
* trusts me
* treats me as an equal
* respects my family
* understands my need for time alone or with family
* accepts me as I am

These are the qualities of a healthy relationship. Take care these can be misused.

You DESERVE a healthy relationship
GROOMING PREVENTION INITIATIVE

Created by
SOROPTIMIST INTERNATIONAL
OF YORKSHIRE for

Loves me not ...

* is jealous
* is possessive
* tries to control me
* gets violent, loses temper quickly
* always blames me
* is sexually demanding
* keeps me from seeing my friends and family
* makes all the decisions
* embarrasses me in front of others
* hits me
* makes me cry
* makes me feel afraid
* is always "checking up" on me
* takes my money and other things
* threatens to leave me if I don't do what I'm told
* teases, bullies and puts me down

If you recognise even one of these warning signs, you or someone you know may be a victim of abuse ...

You are not alone ...
Call for help now!

Appendix 3: Brain games

Brain rules

Rule 1: We cannot be calm and anxious at the same time. The body provides us with the tools that enable us to calm down, if we have feelings of anxiety.

Rule 2: Anxious feelings are created in the emotional brain, which is located in the right brain hemisphere. Our rational, logical thinking is carried out in the left brain hemisphere. If we experience a flood of emotions, it can drown logical, rational thoughts.

Rule 3: With repetition it can take 3 weeks to break an old habit (good and bad), 6 weeks to make a new habit and 36 weeks to hardwire a habit. The more we do it, the quicker the brain will learn – so, keep practising.

Breathing techniques

Option 1

Sit down comfortably, or possibly lie down. Concentrate on your breathing. The *out* breath stimulates the relaxation response in your body and brain, so try to start with an out breath.

If you have been hyperventilating over something, you may have to force yourself to do an out breath, but it will work to stimulate the relaxation response. The *in* breath stimulates the arousal response. When you breathe out, try and make it as long as you can. Count slowly as you breathe out. Try to count to seven, or say the word 're-lax-at-ion'.

Breathe in. Again, count this breath – it needs to be shorter than the out breath. Or say 'peace' under your breath.

When they start, most people can count five on the in breath.

Breathe in through your nose and draw your breath down into the area just below your navel, allowing your stomach to expand as you breathe and filling your lungs entirely with each breath, before exhaling through your nose. Your stomach should rise, not your chest.

Repeat this as many times as you like, or feel you need to. If you do it long enough, you may fall asleep. The aim is to reach the count of eleven on the out breath, and seven on the in breath – but this is not essential. What is essential is that the out breath is *always* longer than the in breath.

Close your eyes and keep your focus on your breathing, but also notice how feelings of relaxation have started to spread around your body. People feel relaxation differently, so you may find your arms or legs becoming lighter or heavier, maybe your fingers or toes become tingly or numb – but you can feel more relaxed now.

Use the out breath to let go of any tension, worries, concerns or pain. You deserve it. You now can do anything calming that your mind would like to do. Maybe you can imagine walking or relaxing in a special place. Identify the sights, smells, sounds, even tastes and textures. Or perhaps you may like instead to imagine listening to a piece of relaxing music, or being bathed in a calming, healing colour – a colour that can reach every part of your mind and body.

You can enjoy this state for 1, 5, 10 or 20 minutes. Whenever you are ready, you can open your eyes, feeling calmer and more relaxed.

The trick to this technique is to practise it repeatedly.

Warning: Most people are aware of the expression, 'Take a deep breath'. I have known people who were feeling angry and told to take a deep breath and then became even angrier. An in breath stimulates the arousal response, so on its own it could make things worse. The exercise is to always take a slow, deep breath in, and then breathe out even more slowly.

Option 2

1. Look at one of your hands. Open it out.

2. Imagine you are placing a present problem into the palm of the hand.

3. Bring your hand right up to your face, so that your palm is touching your eyes.

4. Notice that all you can see is your problem. The light has nearly gone and very little else can be seen.

5. Take a long, slow in breath, count to five, and breathe out.

6. Now slowly withdraw your hand from your face. Keep going with the slow, deep breaths.

7. Stop and notice that you can see your fingers, maybe some rings, also your arm. Be aware that light is showing around your hand and arm.

8. Now take the hand further back. Notice that it is connected to other parts of your body. Look at the clothes you are wearing, or your skin if you are unclothed.

9. Take your hand down to the side of your body and look at the palm of your hand. Look at the problem in the palm of your hand.

Distraction

The '30-second mind changer' forces emotional arousal down by engaging in left-brain activity. This can be a mental exercise, such as listing things alphabetically, learning poetry, mental arithmetic, spelling backwards, reading backwards or translating something into another language. It can be done anywhere at any time.

The '20-minute mind changer' delays making a decision for 20 minutes. Go and do something else completely different for no less than 20 minutes. Creative and/or mental sorting activities work well: for example, playing or writing music, crosswords, writing stories, painting, cooking, puzzle books, gardening, craft work or computer games.

The '90-minute minder': the brain needs to take a break around every 90 minutes. Break away from concentrated work around every 90 minutes for at least 20 to 30 minutes.

Appendix 4: Emotional growth chart

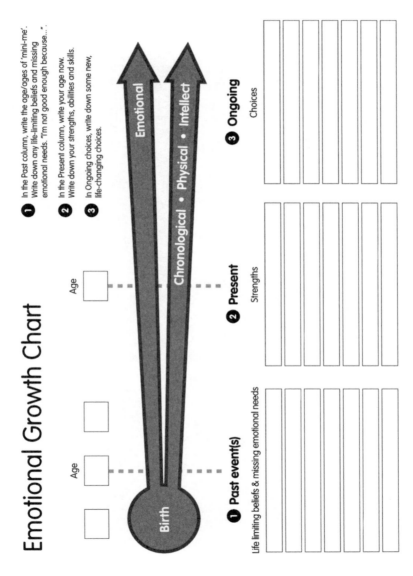

Emotional Growth Chart

1 Past event(s)
Life limiting beliefs & missing emotional needs

2 Present
Strengths

3 Ongoing
Choices

Age

Birth

Emotional

Chronological • Physical • Intellect

1 In the Past column, write the age/ages of 'mini-me'. Write down any life-limiting beliefs and missing emotional needs. "I'm not good enough because…".

2 In the Present column, write your age now. Write down your strengths, abilities and skills.

3 In Ongoing choices, write down some new, life-changing choices.

© Alison Russell 2013

Bibliography

Richard P Bentall, *Doctoring the Mind: Why psychiatric treatments fail* [Paperback] June 2010
ISBN-10: 0141023694   ISBN-13: 978-0141023694

Brandon Bays, *The Journey*. Beyond Words Publishing, 2001.

Peter R. Breggin, *Medication Madness*. St Martin's Press, 2009.

Michael Bywater, *Big Babies: Or: Why Can't We Just Grow Up?* Granta Books, 2007.

Tanith Carey, *Never Kiss in a Canoe: Words of Wisdom from the Golden Age of Agony Aunts*. Boxtree, 2009.

Miriam Chachamu, *How to Calm a Challenging Child*. Foulsham, 2008.

Felicity Davis, *Guard a Silver Sixpence*. Pan, 2011.

Alan de Botton, *Status Anxiety*. Penguin, 2004.

John Duffy, *The Available Parent: Radical Optimism for Raising Teens and Tweens*. Viva Editions, 2011.

Ben Goldacre, *Bad Pharma*. Fourth Estate, 2012.

Daniel Goleman, *Emotional Intelligence*. Bantam, 1996.

Joe Griffin and Ivan Tyrrell, *Dreaming Reality*. HG Publishing, 2006.

Joe Griffin and Ivan Tyrrell (eds), *An Idea in Practice: Using the Human Givens Approach*. HG Publishing, 2007.

Patrick Holford, *Optimum Nutrition for the Mind*. Piatkus, 2003.

Oliver James, *They F*** You Up: How to Survive Family Life* (2nd rev. edn). Bloomsbury, 2006.

Nick Leeson with Ivan Tyrrell, *Back from the Brink: Coping with Stress*. Virgin Books, 2005.

Anne Moir and David Jessel, *Brain Sex: The Real Difference Between Men and Women*. Delta, 1992.

Colin Robson, *Real World Research* (3rd edn). John Wiley & Sons, 2011.

Dorothy Rowe, *Dorothy Rowe's Guide to Life*. HarperCollins, 1996.

David Servan-Schreiber, *Healing without Freud or Prozac: Natural Approaches to Curing Stress, Anxiety and Depression*. Rodale, 2011.

Martin E.P. Seligman, *Authentic Happiness*. Atria Books, 2004.

Joe Simpson, *Touching the Void*. Vintage, 1998.

Marcus Trescothick, *Coming Back To Me*. Harper Sport, 2009.

Simon Baron-Cohen , *The Essential Difference*. Penguin 2004

Ivan Tyrrell and Joe Griffin, *How to Master Anxiety*. HG Publishing, 2006.

Pauline Wallin, *Taming Your Inner Brat: A Guide for Transforming Self-Defeating Behavior*. Beyond Words Publishing, 2001.

Marianne Williamson, *A Return to Love: Reflections on the Principle of 'A Course in Miracles'*. Thorsons, 1996.

Robert Winston, *The Human Mind*. Chartered Institute of Personnel and Development, 2006.

Dorothy Law Nolte (Author), Rachel Harris (Author), *Children Learn What They Live* Publisher: Workman. Publishing; Re-issue edition (26 Jun 1998) ISBN-10: 0761109196 ISBN-13: 978-0761109198

Reprinted with the permission of Beyond Words/Atria Publishing Group from THERE'S A HOLE IN MY SIDEWALK: THE ROMANCE OF SELF-DISCOVERY by Portia Nelson. Copyright © 1993 by Portia Nelson. All rights reserved.

Andrew Baker, 'Marcus Trescothick's autobiography relates nature of depression with brutal honesty'. *Telegraph*, 26 November 2008. Available at: www.telegraph.co.uk/sport/cricket/3527898/Marcus-Trescothicks-award-winning-autobiography-relates-nature-of-depression-with-brutal-honesty-Cricket.html

Claire Dyer, 'City worker bullied by "mean and spiteful" colleagues wins £817,000'. *Guardian*, 2 August 2006. Available at: www.theguardian.com/business/2006/aug/02/genderissues.uknews

Mark Easton, 'Is England a nation on anti-depressants?'. *BBC News*, 3 August 2013. Available at: www.bbc.co.uk/news/uk-23553897

Bret S. Stetka, MD, Christoph U. Correll, MDDisclosures May 21, 2013 www.medscape.com

Richard Eden, 'Paediatrician attack: "People don't want no paedophiles here"'. *Telegraph*, 3 September 2000. Available at: www.telegraph.co.uk/news/uknews/1353904/Paediatrician-attack-People-dont-want-no-paedophiles-here.html

Rebecca Hardy, 'Gary Lineker: There aren't any skeletons in my closet'. *Daily Mail*, 8 March 2013. Available at: www.dailymail.co.uk/femail/article-2289692/Gary-Lineker-fears-Paul-Gascoigne-wild-rumours-private-life.htm

Johann Hari, 'Do I really need this artificial happiness?' *The Independent*, 10 August 2006. Available at: www.independent.co.uk/voices/commentators/johann-hari/johann-hari-do-i-really-need-this-artificial-happiness-411218.html

Clive James, Smoking: My lost love. *A Point of View*, BBC, 3 August 2007. Available at: http://news.bbc.co.uk/1/hi/magazine/6929670.stm

Jenny Johnston, 'Gabby's still furious… just don't tell her our friends voted for me, says Kenny Logan'. *Daily Mail*, 1 December 2007. Available at: www.dailymail.co.uk/tvshowbiz/article-498812/Gabbys-furious--just-dont-tell-friends-voted-says-Kenny-Logan.html

James Lawton, 'The Open 2013: "Brain dead" Rory McIlroy admits he needs help after dreadful 79'. *The Independent*, 19 July 2013. Available at: www.independent.co.uk/sport/golf/the-open-2013-brain-dead-rory-mcilroy-admits-he-needs-help-after-dreadful-79-8718497.html

Mind, 'Landmark moment as antidepressant prescriptions top 50 million'. 30 July 2013. Available at: www.mind.org.uk/news/9310_landmark_moment_as_antidepressant_prescriptions_top_50_million

John Naish, 'Ritalin calms hyperactive children and prescriptions are soaring – but experts warn of serious side-effects and it's even being linked to suicide'. *Daily Mail*, 8 May 2002. Available at: www.dailymail.co.uk/health/article-2141044/ADHD-Ritalin-prescriptions-soaring-experts-warn-effects.html

John Powell, 'Guidelines on touch: Making contact'. *Nursery World*, 11 April 2001. Available at: www.nurseryworld.co.uk/article/722359/guidelines-touch-making-contact

James Rampton, 'Profile. Maxine Peake: Truly shameless', *The Independent*, 27 February 2007. Available at: www.britmovie.co.uk/forums/actors-actresses/85391-maxine-peake-truly-shameless.html

The Northern Echo, 'Failed fledglings – curse or blessing?' 24 May 2013. Available at: www.thenorthernecho.co.uk/features/columnists/latest/10442268.Failed_fledglings____curse_or_blessing_/

The Economist, 'Does psychiatry medicalise too many normal behaviours?' 17 May 2013. Available at: www.economist.com/economist-asks/does-psychiatry-medicalise-too-many-normal-behaviours

York Press, 'Stiletto shoe fetish man, Jess Collinson, is jailed for 16 months'. 5 March 2013. Available at: www.yorkpress.co.uk/news/10266699.Stiletto_shoe_fetish_man_jailed/

Laura Topham, '[Maureen Nolan:] Bernie's cancer taught me that you must live life to the full'. *Daily Mail*, 11 May 2013. Available at: www.dailymail.co.uk/health/article-2322948/Bernies-cancer-taught-live-life-means-beating-deafness-Maureen-Nolan-reveals-sisters-fight-inspired-begin-own.html

Useful links

Brainsex: www.brainsexmatters.com

Emotional Freedom Technique (EFT):
www.emotional-health.co.uk

Emotional Needs Audit (ENA) project:
www.enaproject.org

Hidden Talents:
http://en.wikipedia.org/wiki/Hidden_Talent

PTSD Resolution (for armed forces, reservists and their
families): www.ptsdresolution.org

Self-development: www.uncommon-knowledge.co.uk

in8 Cards - therapeutic teaching tools using innate skills
to enrich life. www.in8uk.com

Alison R. Russell:
Web: www.chasingrainbows.org.uk
Facebook: Alison R. Russell
Twitter: @chasingbows
Audiobook: Alisonrussell
LinkedIn: Alison R. Russell
Email: Alisonrussell@chasingrainbows.org.uk